The Pollak is an incredibl⟨...⟩ ences. Imagine putting a⟨...⟩ big table. Now picture laying a sheet of transparent plastic over it, like the sheets teachers used to use for overhead projectors. Make marks, maybe little "x"s, on that sheet with a blue pen, for visual sightings of apparitions. Now take another sheet and lay it on top, and mark audio phenomena in red pen. Do the same thing with another sheet of plastic and a yellow pen for the phantom smells people have experienced in different parts of the building. Use an orange pen for when people have been touched. Maybe choose a green pen to mark where EVPs have been recorded. Use a purple pen to note just random weirdness. When you're finished, you're going to have a rainbow of "x"s all over the building's footprint. Supernatural phenomena happen in every single part of this building, and what happens involves every one of the senses – every single one, including, for some, the sixth sense.

I don't know if it's because the building is constantly being used for research except for the months of August through October, when the haunt is built and presented. Maybe the spirits congregate there because of all the investigative and haunt activity. Or maybe it's because people are actively searching for paranormal evidence there, and occurrences in other asylum buildings go unreported (but not unnoticed). Whatever the reason, the Pollak fairly hums with spectral activity.

FRACTURED SOULS

BY SYLVIA SHULTS

*Historical Information and Documentation
provided by
Christina Morris, Curator of the Peoria State Hospital Museum*

TABLE OF CONTENTS

FOREWORD

BY DALE KACZMAREK

A huge complex of buildings, hospitals, cottages and other structures once existed in the small town of Bartonville, Illinois. Just about five miles from downtown Peoria, these buildings once housed what would later become Peoria State Hospital. Throughout the years these buildings were repurposed and many razed to make room for newer structures. Some still remain today and at least two were used for paranormal overnight investigations; the Bowen Building and Pollak Hospital.

In the early days of psychiatric medicine many state psychiatric hospitals were archaic and often downright abusive in the way that they handled their patients. Frontal lobotomies, electro-shock therapy, ice-water immersion bath techniques as well as isolation cells, chaining or restraining patients to their beds or the walls, even the use of Utica cribs. In the latter, a patient was literally imprisoned within a very small horizontal area without much room to maneuver, turn over or move at all. Is it no wonder that quite a number of these former facilities are haunted today by those patients that were treated so poorly?

It wasn't necessarily the doctors or staff's fault as those techniques were state-of-the-art at the time. Today, though, they are deemed unnecessary or hurtful. All these types of treatments were nullified by Dr. Zeller who said that patients should be treated as family and not subjected to those kinds of actions or restraints. Dr. Zeller advanced psychiatric medicine several generations and received many accolades for his humane treatment of patients in the Peoria State Hospital complex.

The former Bowen Building, now gone forever, was a teaching facility and not a hospital where any procedures were performed, even though some have said that, in the past, atrocious hospital procedures, lobotomies and autopsies were conducted in the basement as well as other parts of the hospital, which simply isn't true. Talk of suicides by hanging from a staircase is also just a fabrication. Even without all of the hype, the building was considered to be quite haunted.

The Ghost Research Society had the opportunity of investigating this building twice; once in 2012 and again in 2015. We did uncover some amazing evidence including the sounds of barefoot running feet, female screams, disembodied voices and the sounds of pebbles being thrown at investigators.

The other building still being used for paranormal investigations is the Pollak Hospital which was a tuberculosis hospital where an average of four to five people died a day! Surely this is the building where a lot more paranormal activity is possible and has been gathered by a number of paranormal groups including the Ghost Research Society. We investigated this location in September of 2015 where some amazing video footage was captured in the Men's Death Ward. A white sheet-like appendage suddenly loomed out of the darkness behind and to the right of our guide, Christina Morris. This weird aberration appeared soon after Morris was talking about having to bind some patient's corpses in tight sheets before the bodies were sent home to family.

Besides the visual phenomena captured, there were plenty of EVPs (Electronic Voice Phenomena) as well as disembodied sounds and words produced by the Ovilus X. The Pollak Hospital is far more haunted than the former Bowen Building. This building is "infested" with spirits!

This all leads us to the author of this fine book, Sylvia Shults. I met Sylvia quite a number of years ago and she immediately impressed me as a person interested in discovering the truth of the Peoria State Hospital complex. She has an intense interest in the paranormal as well as the history and genealogy of those who were once patients here. Through her never-ending research, she has been able to dispel many of the urban legends, falsehoods, undocumented gossip and even outright untruths about Peoria State Hospital. Her tireless search for the truth has uncovered and set the record straight to many of those "tales" that were told throughout the years.

Sylvia's books are the kind that once you pick them up and begin to read, you cannot put them down without finishing them. They are just that addictive. She is not just a historian and researcher but likes to investigate these and other locations for that very personal encounter with something supernatural. So, in reading this book, the reader will come away with a unique angle of both history and the paranormal. I have always said that history and hauntings go hand in hand. One must understand and digest the history of a location before one can fully grasp the paranormal episodes and determine any possible connection. There is usually something in the past history of any location that may have precipitated the ghost event. Most times, a ghost or spirit haunts a location due to some form of untimely death; i.e. murder, suicide, etc. I personally believe that in the case of Peoria State Hospital's many spirits, they continue to be perceived here probably due to the fact that they were treated so well and are reliving their last few months or years at a place that they might have called home. Strong powerful emotions can leave a psychic imprint or "place memory" embedded in the fabric of time and space and under certain conditions that we do not fully understand, these are replayed to the observer in the form of either visual or audio phenomena. Understanding the history is essential in understanding the psychic phenomena.

This is where someone like Sylvia comes into play.

She will overwhelm you with the past; which is a good thing by the way, so that the reader can make that psychic connection. This is not just a book of ghost stories but also the most complete compilation of Peoria State Hospital's past ever told! She is so very passionate about this location and that passion comes through if you've ever had a chance to see Sylvia speak at a public presentation. Watching her talk is a pleasure and the reader will learn so much more when they read Fractured Souls and the first volume in the series, Fractured Spirits. Her connection to Peoria State Hospital is so intense that one can sometimes see her tear up a bit, especially when relating the story of Rhoda Derry who suffered so much before becoming a patient here. It is a very powerful and emotional story!

This is one book that you cannot pass up. Fractured Spirits already holds a special place on my bookshelf and it should absolutely be in your collection as well. The history is outstanding and the many ghost stories and investigations will keep you on the edge of your seat throughout. If you are thinking of purchasing any book on the paranormal in the future, put this book at the top of your list. You won't be disappointed.

And if you are ever in the Peoria, Illinois area, do stop and take a walk back in time on "The Hilltop". You might just come across a wispy figure of a former patient still wandering the grounds or hear a gentle whisper carried by the breeze of a beautiful summer's afternoon. You aren't going crazy; you've probably just made a connection to the other side!

Dale Kaczmarek is the president of Ghost Research Society and director of Excursions Into the Unknown, Inc., hosting ghost tours of haunted Chicagoland locations since 1982. Kaczmarek has been actively investigating ghosts, hauntings, and poltergeist phenomena since 1975 and is active in a number of organizations, including American Association for Electronic Voice Phenomena, Society of the Investigation of the Unexplained, International Fortean Organization, and the prestigious Ghost Club of England. He is CEO of Ghost Research Society Press, publishing fine books on paranormal and mysterious phenomena since 2004.

INTRODUCTION

The Jehovah's Witness who periodically stops by my house to see about the state of my soul happened to come by when I was working on this book. He's always pleasant, always starts off his conversation by asking me how I'm doing, so I told him I was working on a second book about the Peoria State Hospital. His witnessing partner, an elegant platinum blonde in a stylish cardinal red wool coat, gave a shiver that had nothing to do with the 15-degree weather on the porch.

"Bartonville!" she muttered. She flashed me a quick smile.

"When I was a kid, I thought the entire town was crazy. You know, because that's how everybody referred to the state hospital—'Bartonville'."

The man nodded. "My grandfather was in there. He had a nervous breakdown, and that's where they sent him. And my mother worked there. She was a clerk-typist."

I shook my head, grinning. "I tell you what, you talk to just about anyone in this area, anyone who grew up here, and they're gonna have a story about the state hospital."

The lady in the red coat piped up brightly, "My aunt ran off with one of the patients." I was aching to ask her to elaborate on *that* story, but the witnessing started, and it was still fifteen degrees out—hardly the right weather to stand out on the porch and beg for stories, as fascinating as they promised to be.

The doors of the Peoria State Hospital closed for the final time in 1973, but you'll be hard-pressed to find a more active place. Now, instead of the shuffle and conversation of patients, and the voices of caregivers briskly giving orders, the hallways of the remaining asylum buildings are much more likely to echo with the noisy blurts of an SB7 spirit box, the beeping of a Rempod, or simply the quiet reverence of paranormal investigators sitting quietly in the dark, waiting to contact the dead.

You see, the past isn't dead at the Peoria State Hospital, and the dead aren't gone. The abandoned asylum is now known across the country as a place where the past still lives, both in well-worn stories and in new experiences. And those experiences are overwhelmingly paranormal in nature.

This book, and its predecessor, *Fractured Spirits*, will challenge what you may have been told over the years about the Peoria State Hospital. You hear "haunted mental asylum", and you assume you know the sordid story so common to other institutions that housed the mentally ill. People who suffer from mental illness inhabit a very confusing and at times frightening world. But the Peoria State Hospital was a place of refuge for the suffering.

Dr. George Zeller, the revered superintendent of the asylum from 1902 to 1935, had a policy in which he proposed to take in "the worst of the worst" patients. A modern mind automatically assumes, oh, you must mean violently psychotic patients. Dr. Zeller's interpretation of that phrase was much different. By "worst of the worst", he meant those patients who could not care for themselves, people that needed the most care, people who were considered incurable, people that every other institution had given up on—the most vulnerable of the mentally ill. That's who he was determined to fill this institution with.

With these stories, I intend to shine light on the shadows of mental illness as it was experienced in one of the most progressive institutions in the world. Many people don't realize this, but central Illinois was on the cutting edge of new breakthroughs in research on the care and treatment of the mentally ill. The nonrestraint and humane care at the Peoria State Hospital, the drug research in the labs at Galesburg Mental Health Center—this was all happening right here in central Illinois.

The Peoria State Hospital was also far, far ahead of its time in another area: the way the female staff was empowered. The asylum had the finest nursing college in the country for thirty-six years, and even after that program ended, training continued. Young women were trained to take care of the most vulnerable members of society. In the course of this education, these women became independent. They could make their own way in the world, they could support themselves with their skills, they could train others. That was a big deal in the early part of the twentieth century. Women couldn't even vote, and yet, here they were, running the most compassionate institution for the care of the mentally ill in the *world*.

There have been a lot of changes on the hilltop in the past few years. We lost the iconic Bowen Building, but we gained a museum. The Peoria State Hospital Museum is now located in the firehouse. Those of us interested in the history of the asylum are still learning the details about life in this fascinating place. There's seventy-one years of history to digest here, from 1902 to 1973. The museum gives us the perfect environment in which to learn. Christina Morris, historian of the Peoria State Hospital and curator of the museum, will readily admit that she herself continues to learn about the asylum.

I'll give you a perfect example of this. When I was working on *Fractured Spirits*, Christina told me about student nurses performing autopsies at the Bowen, as part of their training. She has since learned that it was doctors that did autopsies, not student nurses. And these autopsies took place in the basements of the hospitals, not the Bowen Building. The nurses did dissection of body parts, as part of their education into the mysteries of human anatomy. A dissection is a teaching tool. An autopsy, on the other hand, is an investigation undertaken by a doctor, a quest to discover cause of death. That is *not* within the wheelhouse of a student nurse. It's an important distinction.

The museum is a valuable resource for historical research. Paranormal research, meanwhile, continues at the Pollak Hospital. People still come to the asylum's cemeteries, either to find their own lost loved ones, or to visit one or both of our two most beloved asylum characters, Bookbinder and Rhoda Derry. And all over the grounds, the spirits of the Peoria State Hospital still remind us of their quiet presence.

Serious paranormal investigators know how important it

is to know the history of a place. This knowledge can direct your investigation, leading you to ask questions that will get better responses from the spirits. A familiarity with the history of a haunted place can also help explain the local legends that crop up around the area. We'll see a lot of this in the upcoming pages. So many of the paranormal stories of the asylum can actually be backed up by the historical record. For my money, that makes the stories more interesting. When you can trace a ghost story back to its source, that really brings home the fact that it *happened to someone*. It brings the personal element to the ghost stories, and that makes the tales so much more vital.

It's a fascinating exercise, matching story to history. Here's just one example to whet your appetite: Sophie Zeller, one of the candidates for our resident Lady in White, died in October 1937. And the Lady in White that hangs out near the Bowen Building is most often seen ... in October. When you hear hoofbeats, you don't look for zebras. You look for horses.

I'm delighted to say that this second installment of tales from the asylum, like its predecessor, also has links to video evidence and audio recordings. Several ghost hunting groups have been generous enough to share their evidence with the world on YouTube. I'll direct you guys right to it. Just like in *Fractured Spirits*, wherever you see a little ghostie icon, like this: 👻 that's your hint that there's fun stuff waiting for you on the Internet. Type in the link, or visit the Fractured Spirits page on Facebook, or visit my website at: http://www.sylviashults.wordpress.com. I'll post the links there too. I will make sure you can find this extraordinary evidence, because it's just too good to miss.

This second book also gives me the chance to correct some, um, misunderstandings. For example, in the interest of continually striving for refinement and accuracy in the stories I bring you, I should mention this: in *Fractured Spirits*, I wrote that Rhoda Derry was carried in a basket up the hillside stairs. I have since learned that the staircase that winds up the forested slope of the hill was installed in the 1930s, decades after Rhoda's arrival. "Being carried up the hill", in Rhoda's case, refers to the gentle slope between the train platform on the hilltop and the cottages in C Row.

(And speaking of trains and their destinations, that has also been a source of some confusion in the past. The train station—was it at the bottom of the hill, or at the top? Well, actually ... both. There was a train station at the bottom of the hill. An electric train used to run between Peoria and Pekin, with a stop in Bartonville. Steam trains also pulled into that station. Passengers disembarked there, and continued on their way by buggy or, later, by car. Meanwhile, rail cars containing supplies for the asylum, and new patient arrivals, decoupled from the main part of the train and continued up the hill to the platform. The remnants of the platform are very near the base of the water tower.)

Furthermore, the aforementioned staircase in the woods was only for use by asylum staff and personnel. That particular route down the hillside was off-limits to patients.

This doesn't mean the staircase got no use. It got plenty of use. Much of that foot traffic was nurses sneaking down after hours to visit bars along the river, like the Blue Gardens.

Also in the interest of refinement and accuracy, I am sorry to say that many of the stories reported to me about the Bowen Building, stories that I included in *Fractured Spirits*, turned out to be tall tales. I tried at the time to convey this with language like "They say..." and "Some people have claimed ...", but let me make it clear: some of those tales were told to me by people who were misinformed, or worse, who simply invented their own "facts".

I'll even put in a disclaimer right up front here for this book. When you're collecting stories about the paranormal, and you are relying on the impressions of others, details can sometimes get a little woolly. In fact, that's said to be the hallmark of an actual paranormal experience—if the witness tells the story more than once, the basic details should not change. The experience, if it truly was paranormal, is likely to be seared into the witness's psyche.

But witnesses put their own spin on things. They can't help it. And when you're talking about a haunted mental institution, with that added spooky stigma, things get even weirder. Some

of these stories, I heard from two or three different people—
which means two or three different viewpoints. Any mistakes
in the details are mine alone. I tried my best to distill every dis-
parate version into a story that was true—and coherent.

I am not in the habit of pooh-poohing people's experiences—far from it. But I've come to realize that the Bowen ...
well, the Bowen cast a spell over the people who experienced
her. And as you'll see in the next chapter, sometimes that spell
made people's imaginations run a little wild.

RUMORS AND TRUTHS

"My favorite so far is the one about the groundskeeper who killed a bunch of little girls."

Christina Morris and I were at the Peoria State Hospital Museum. The 2018 Christmas Sock Hop was in full swing, and people were milling around, sipping sodas and munching on Doritos. Someone had brought a birthday cake, and it was already half gone. The teenage haunt volunteers can do serious damage to a table of party food.

"They said he murdered children of people who worked here. I mean, come *on*. Those two guys who got scalded to death? One of them, there were twenty-two newspaper articles written just about him. If you had some groundskeeper up here killing little girls, it'd have been all over the papers!"

I nodded. I was familiar with the story: in the early days of the asylum's operation, when they were still getting used to the steam heat technology, two male patients who were getting hydrotherapy treatments were accidentally scalded in their tubs. Nurses oversaw the hydrotherapy, but it was other patients who stood by and actually manipulated the hot and cold water faucets coming into the tubs. They weren't properly trained, and they got over-zealous with the hot water. Yes, it was a tragedy, but Dr. Zeller owned it. There was no cover-up.

"I still shake my head at the Model T story." In the 1920s or 30s, so the tale goes, a nurse was standing at the attic window of the Bowen Building watching a car drive up Pfeiffer Road, a car driven by her husband with her young child in it. As she watched, the car exploded, killing both her husband and her child. The nurse was so distraught at witnessing this, she threw herself from the window, committing suicide.

Christina laughed. "Yeah, right. Explain to me how a Model T—or any car—can just randomly explode."

"Not to mention, how could it drive up Pfeiffer Road in the 1930s, when the road wasn't even put in until the 1980s?"

"Plus, if she'd thrown herself out of the window and landed in the street, it would have been pretty hard for her to miss the *porch roof*. You know, the roof of the porches that encircled the building? You'd have to really launch yourself in order to clear those and land in the street."

We laughed together, but the sad fact is that she and I are still both fighting the misinformation, questionable history, and outright lies that still sneak around the hilltop.

And we're not alone. Even when Dr. Zeller was in charge, rumors were raising their ugly heads, and then as now, it took a good healthy dose of common sense to combat them. In his autobiography, Dr. Zeller writes that the State Board in Springfield had heard "that a reign of terror existed in our neighborhood and that our paroled patients were committing all sorts of depredations." The State Board sent a man to investigate. The man spent three days in Bartonville without announcing his presence to Dr. Zeller. After poking around for three days, talking to every resident he could find, he walked into Dr. Zeller's office and confessed his surprise. "He came expecting to find an excited and hostile community, but after visiting numerous homes and interviewing many people, he found that our methods were heartily approved of and not one uttered a word of hostile criticism..."

Unfortunately, nowadays, a great many of these spurious stories originate in the Bowen Building. The Bowen was the public face of the Peoria State Hospital. Even after the asylum closed its doors, people recognized the Bowen. In fact, many people thought that this one building was the sum total of the hospital—that big stone building on the hilltop, that was it, end of story. That's how iconic it was. Even people who knew there were other buildings were fascinated with the brooding, almost Gothic bulk of the Bowen. It looked as if it had every right to be haunted ... and people supplied their own horror stories to go along with the big spooky building on the hilltop.

I was at a paranormal conference in Rockford when renowned investigator Dale Kaczmarek gave a presentation that included evidence his team had captured at the Bowen Building. In his talk, he spoke of a strange EVP his team had recorded in the basement of the building.

"We were down in the autopsy room, and we caught what sounded like a young woman giggling. We just couldn't figure out why we caught that in the morgue."

Here's the thing about paranormal investigators: we try our best to find reasons for what we experience, but sometimes, we run up against the inexplicable. When that happens, we say, "Dude, that's just weird," and we move on. But in this case, I did have an explanation.

I caught up with Dale at his table after his talk. After telling him how much I enjoyed it—because I always dig people talking about the Peoria State Hospital—I said, "Hey, if you're interested, I can tell you why you captured a giggle in the basement of the Bowen."

He raised an eyebrow, so I plunged ahead. We've talked with nurses who actually took classes at the Bowen, or did their psych residence at the asylum. They told stories about sneaking out of their rooms at night. What had been pointed out to Dale as the autopsy room ... was actually a pantry. We've heard tales of student nurses sneaking down to the pantry after lights out to snag cans of peaches to enjoy in their room. Illicitly-gotten fruit can sometimes be the sweetest.

"So that giggle you heard," I told Dale, "that was the sound of a little nurse getting away with something!"

Dale was charmed. "You know, that makes a lot more sense."

After years of visiting the Peoria State Hospital, and interacting with the spirits there, I firmly believe that there is nothing truly malevolent there. There just isn't. The spirits on the hilltop are just that—the spirits of people who came to the asylum to find relief from their problems, whether they suffered from mental or physical illness. Even the "bully" spirit in the basement of the Pollak Hospital has proven to be simply a gruff electrician who wants to be left alone to get on with his work, rather

than be bothered by ghost hunters traipsing around "his" basement. All these stories of people getting hurt, shoved, scratched,
having their nose broken—I now believe these are simply fabri-
cations, yet one more instance of people being afraid of things
they don't yet understand.

Let's face it—when you say the words "haunted mental asylum", your mind goes all American Horror Story on you, and
you automatically assume that the place was a snake pit of pain,
fear, and abuse. It is my privilege to tell people that this was
not the case at the Peoria State Hospital. I still take every story
I hear at face value, and I always will, out of respect for the
person telling it. I will never publicly sneer at someone's story,
because it is their story to tell.

But—and here's where time and experience and knowledge
make all the difference—these days, if I hear someone tell me
that they got hurt or attacked by an evil entity at the asylum, or
that the doctors tortured the patients, or that the nurses used to
line the male patients up in the hallway and force them to mas-
turbate, I will nod, look serious, and then ignore pretty much
everything they've just told me. Because they've probably just
made it up to have a "good story" to tell. And yes, I've heard
every one of these stories, and more besides.

(Even Shane Cleer, who shared his story of getting scratched
with me for *Fractured Spirits*, said to me recently, "I wish I hadn't
shared that story with you." So I asked him if he had another
experience he'd rather share, and as it turned out, he did. His
story is in a later chapter.)

It seems that the most insidious misinformation arises from
the Bowen Building. Of *course* the tragic nurse who watched
a car explode for no good reason threw herself from the attic
window of the Bowen. A freaky schizophrenic menacing White
Lady? You'll find her at the Bowen. Satanic rituals and demonic
entities? Check the basement of the Bowen. And the "hanging
tree" in the woods, where patients were committing suicide by
the dozens? You guessed it—right across the street from the
Bowen. (Every one of those stories is fake news, by the way.)

I think I've figured out why the Bowen is such a magnet
for tall tales. The Bowen was the most iconic of the asylum

buildings. It's the one most people picture when they hear the words "Peoria State Hospital". And some of the guides who worked there may have felt the need to embellish their stories just a bit, to give people on the tours what the guides thought they wanted. After all, these folks paid for a look at a haunted mental asylum. And a haunted mental asylum must be just a hotbed of abuse and torture, right?

And sometimes, these whoppers arose from nothing more than a simple breakdown of communication. Let me give you an example.

On a Bowen tour, it was inevitable that you would arrive at a certain room on the second floor. This room was pretty neat: it had big windows that let in plenty of natural light. Interestingly, the room was divided by a wall that featured a couple of wide windows, reinforced with chicken wire. The guides running your tour would tell you, with a perfectly straight face, that this was the room where the lobotomies were performed. And when a procedure was botched (which, the guides hinted, was most of the time), the nurses and doctors performing the lobotomy would scurry behind the door, behind the safety of the reinforced windows, lock the door behind them, and watch through the windows as the patient bled out and died, right in front of them.

Let's unpack this, shall we?

First of all, let's look at some facts about lobotomies in general. There were two kinds of lobotomies. The prefrontal lobotomy was the earlier, original form of the procedure, in which the doctor went in through the temple to get to the prefrontal lobe of the patient's brain. The later, easier, way more popular procedure was the transorbital lobotomy. In this version, also known gruesomely as the "icepick" lobotomy, the doctor would work a thin pointy instrument (okay, fine, an icepick) into the inner corner of the patient's eye, nudging the eyeball aside. Then he would punch through the thin bone at the back of the eye socket, work the pick up, then down, and withdraw the pick. That's it—the operation was done. (This is the operation made popular by Dr. Walter Freeman, who performed hundreds of them, going cross-country in his endearingly named

Lobotomobile. And I am not even remotely making this up.)

My point is, there is no blood involved in a transorbital lobotomy. None. It was actually far less invasive than the prefrontal version. At worst, the patient would have a black eye. And this was the later, preferred version of the lobotomy. By the time any lobotomies were performed on the hilltop, this was the procedure they were doing. We'll get to that in just a moment.

After the nursing college closed in the 1930s, the Nurses' Building (what we now know as the Bowen) became the administration building. This particular room, once a nurses' lounge, had a partial wall installed, and was used to store patient records and prescription pads. *That* was the reason for the lockable door, and the windows reinforced with chicken wire.

And here's the kicker: if you stand in this room, and you *look out the window,* you can see where the Levitin and Talcott Hospitals used to stand, before they were torn down in the mid-1980s. (Pfeiffer Road was put in at around the same time. The road goes through the basements of the buildings, which is why some ghosts are seen along the road. They're still wandering the halls of a building that no longer exists.) Levitin Hospital was the infirmary for male patients, while Talcott served female patients. And *that* is where the very few lobotomies were performed. Only about ninety patients at the Peoria State Hospital underwent lobotomies. The doctors here realized that this procedure was an option of last resort, and that outcomes were usually bad. Not "death" bad, but quite often a bubbly, outgoing person would be rendered a monotone, childlike zombie by a lobotomy. And these operations happened in the 1940s, well after Dr. Zeller had passed on. When the practice fell out of favor in the 1950s, the doctors at the asylum stopped performing them.

Here's what actually happened. Christina Morris was, at one time, in charge of giving tours through the Bowen, by virtue of her encyclopedic knowledge of the asylum's history. She made a series of flash cards, with historical talking points, and handed them out to the other guides to use. Over time, though, those handy cards got lost or thrown away, and the information on them became twisted and garbled. By that time, Christina had left the Bowen, and there was no one to correct the embellishment that was creeping into the tours. Basically, the historical facts got distorted in a game of Telephone.

Now, doesn't that make a lot more sense than tales of doctors performing bloody, vicious operations in the nurses' dormitory?

When Christina Morris was leading tours at the Bowen Building, a television crew from Chicago showed up unannounced one day. They were there to shoot a pilot for a show on strange, spooky and odd wedding destinations. Christina was tapped to lead the crew around as they shot footage.

"They had big cameras, it was a big to-do ... I'm talking, this was a good film crew, we could tell right away. I was in the yard working; I had my work clothes on." Christina took the crew on a walk around the grounds first. As they shot, the guys assured Christina that none of the footage they were shooting would be in the pilot. They simply intended to use shots they were doing of the man and woman playing the engaged couple.

"We started filming, and they realized that wasn't really all that entertaining, so they're like, okay, you be this couple's tour guide. That'll give us more film footage to work with." Christina went along with the director, who decided to do several cut scenes for each part of the tour, getting footage of the same moment from several angles. Again, Christina didn't think anything of it.

They got to the attic, and Christina pointed to the windows. "If you'll notice, we're surrounded by beautiful woodlands," she told the film crew. "Some of these woods were the site of the last, desperate plea of people who wanted to end their lives. We've had several suicides by hanging here on the hilltop."

The camera panned around the room as Christina spoke ... and that's how the disconnect happened.

"Immediately people assumed that the hangings were in the Bowen Building, because I said it, and then they panned around the room! I learned my lesson ... I learned my lesson right then and there."

The pilot never did get made. The director basically cut out the interesting parts—Christina giving her tour—and spliced them together and slapped it up on YouTube. To Christina's everlasting annoyance, that video has been viewed over 90,000 times.

And because of creative editing, it has led to misunderstanding and bad history.

With all this misinformation running rampant in the hallways of the Bowen, it's no wonder that Dale Kaczmarek picked up a very interesting EVP on one of his visits there. Dale and his team were doing the initial walkthrough, and the very young guide was giving them the "history" of the building. (I'm using huge, exaggerated air quotes here.)

As they walked along, listening to the guide's stories, a ghostly voice coughed *"Bullshit."*

THE BOWEN BUILDING

Dr. George Zeller retired in 1935. A grateful Peoria State Hospital board named him Superintendent Emeritus as thanks for his years of service. But one of his colleagues, Archie Bowen, wanted to do something more for Dr. Zeller, something more tangible. Dr. Zeller and his wife, Sophie, were such beloved figures on the hilltop that Mr. Bowen knew they couldn't leave, not yet. So he came to Dr. Zeller with a proposition: would he and Sophie consider moving into one of the apartments in the Nurses' Building?

It took two conversations, but by the end of the second one, Dr. Zeller had grasped what his old friend and colleague was really asking.

"You mean you want me and Sophie to stay here? On the hilltop?" The Zellers had been living in the Superintendent's Cottage, but Archie was offering a permanent arrangement, one that didn't depend on Dr. Zeller's position.

"For as long as you like," Archie replied.

And this military man, he of the stiff upper lip and the fierce dark gaze, who had served his country in the Spanish-American War and devoted his life to militantly defending the dignity of the mentally ill—this man was in humble tears of gratitude that his colleagues and former staff wanted him to stick around. It's not like Dr. Zeller was destitute at the end of his life. He certainly wasn't broke and homeless—far from it. He'd had a great career, he was well-respected, and he was really quite wealthy, with lots of property to his name. In fact, in 1933 he bought Jubilee College and the grounds on which it sat, a total of 93 acres, six miles outside of Peoria. He donated it to the state of Illinois, and it became Jubilee College State Park. He could have lived in any number of fine homes. But he accepted Mr. Bowen's offer because it meant that he and Sophie could live out the rest of their days at the asylum they both loved so much.

He and Sophie moved into an apartment on the second floor, at the end of the building facing what is now Pfeiffer Road. From there, Dr. Zeller could look out over the grounds of his beloved asylum. And that is where Dr. Zeller passed away in 1938.

HISTORY OF THE NURSES' BUILDING

The Employee's Building (aka the Bowen Building).
This view, which many people considered the front of the building, was actually the back. Note the beautiful porches: these porches, at the back of the building, were where the student nurses would take their breaks.

The classes that made up the original three-year nursing program formed the backbone of the very best accredited school of nursing in the country. For over three decades, young women were trained to care for the mentally and physically ill. A few male students were trained as orderlies, but the overwhelming majority of students that sought their education at the Peoria State Hospital were women. And why not? They got a magnificent chance to succeed in a fulfilling career, doing real good in their community. Dr. Zeller even encouraged his nurses to go on to become doctors in their own right. Dr. Zeller believed passionately that women were equal to men, and indeed, were superior when it came to tending to the needs of patients with mental illness. He believed that the gentle touch of a compassionate nurse was far preferable to the rough attitude of a male attendant.

Dr. Zeller, as it turns out, was right. It was not uncommon for patients to wander away from the asylum grounds, due to the no-locked-door policy. Sometimes patients would get as far as Peoria, where they often got picked up by the police. When this happened, the station would simply pick up the phone and dial the asylum. "We've got one of your folks here—please come and collect them." A pretty young nurse would be sent on the train to round up the patient and bring them back to the fold. And the patient would come along quietly, maybe a little abashed that they'd caused so much bother.

In 1936, all state hospital schools of nursing closed. The asylum's unparalleled school shut down in July of that year. But just a few months later, in October, the Peoria State Hospital School of Psychiatric Nursing opened its doors. The school was now affiliated with Methodist Hospital School of Nursing in Peoria and Brokaw Hospital School of Nursing in Normal.

This slight change in direction reflected a changing attitude towards nurses' training. A specialized hospital was no longer considered the ideal training environment for basic nursing. Instead, specialized institutions, like state hospitals, were used for a two-month course in psychiatric nursing, as part of a nurse's undergraduate work. This gave student nurses from three general hospitals in the community a chance to study psychiatric nursing, instead of providing an entire course of study for only the students at the asylum.

In the late 1940s, another course of study, this one lasting eighteen months, was developed for attendants and psychiatric aides. Peoria State Hospital was one of only a few hospitals in the world, and the only one in Illinois, that offered a psychiatric technician program.

These later courses of study never achieved the cachet that Dr. Zeller's original nurses' college did in the early decades of the century. Nevertheless, Peoria State Hospital continued to provide excellent training for nurses and attendants until it closed in 1973.

After the asylum's closing, the Bowen remained, an elegant reminder of dedicated service. But with the passage of decades of Illinois winters, the building began to show her age. The Bowen was a beautiful building, constructed from Indiana limestone (which was actually brought from the oldest quarry in the United States, in Bedford, Indiana). It stood at the crest of the hilltop, a proud silhouette against the blue Illinois sky.

That visibility soon proved to be the Bowen's downfall. After the Peoria State Hospital closed its doors, urban explorers moved in on the abandoned buildings. Sometimes, their intentions weren't as innocuous as taking a few pictures in the name of exploration. The Bowen, with its stone walls and vaguely Gothic bones, suffered the most. The basement was the scene of unspeakable rituals designed to call forth demonic spirits. (Let me make something very clear: I'm not saying there *were* demonic spirits in the basement of the Bowen. I'm saying that misguided, overstimulated people with vivid imaginations and delusions of pseudo-Satanic grandeur performed rituals in the basement in an attempt to summon dark entities. Christina Morris likes to tell of the time she and a friend, as teenagers, were exploring in the Bowen. They knew people had been breaking in to vandalize the place, and they wanted to discourage that. They heard another group in the first floor hallway, muddling through a "Satanic ritual". This was in the 1980s, at the height of the Satanic Panic, so there was a fair bit of this nonsense going on at the Bowen at the time. Christina and her friend did an end run around the group, taking the Pfeiffer Road stairwell to the second floor. They sneaked across the building, then started quietly down the other echoing second floor stairwell, calling out in their spookiest, deepest voices—"*I see-e-e-e you, The Dark Master is co-o-o-m-m-ming!*" The kids scrambled all over each other to be the first out of the building.)

DALE KACZMAREK AND GHOST RESEARCH SOCIETY

Dale Kaczmarek and his group, Ghost Research Society, have visited the Bowen twice. And each time, they have come away with thought-provoking evidence.

On one occasion, the group was watching the camera feeds in Command Central when one of the cameras on the second floor went out. Dale and Stanley Suho went up to the second floor with a fresh battery, just in case. Sure enough, the battery was dead. As soon as Dale got the battery compartment door off, he and Stan both saw a small blob of silvery mist move quickly down the hallway. Dale slapped the fresh battery into the camera, but of course the anomaly was long gone.

(That's one of the most frustrating things about this business. Entities seem to have an uncanny sense of when a camera is temporarily out of service, or is pointing the other way, or—here's the best one—hasn't been turned on yet. They *know*, man.)

Later that same evening, two more investigators, Kathie Para and Marge Sucha, were in the same hallway on the second floor when they saw a small dark entity. They reported that it was black, fuzzy, and about the size of a small dog. It skittered down the hallway as the women lit it up with their flashlight beams, and disappeared before it rounded the corner. To add to the creep factor, the entity moved completely soundlessly. As Dale was telling me about the incident, he said, "You'd have heard claws scratching on the floor, especially with it going so fast. But this thing made no sound *at all*."

(Dale has a theory about this last critter. He feels that as small as it was, and the way it moved so quickly yet noiselessly, it may have been an elemental. Elementals are the usually invisible nature spirits that prowl the edges of human perception. They are also, oddly enough, thought to be attracted to people with mental illness. So, all things considered, I'm inclined to agree with him.)

TAPS

In November 2012, as I was working on *Fractured Spirits*, I was invited to be a part of the Ghost Hunters episode "Prescription For Fear" (Season 9, Episode 3). I will say up front, I'm delighted to have been asked, and I appreciated the opportunity to make an appearance on such a prestigious show.

That being said …

Okay, you *know* I'm going to have an opinion on this. I know, I know, they have to make it spooky to pump up the ratings. But I have a couple of issues with the … creative editing they used in the show. As I was watching the show when it first aired on the SyFy Channel, I was bouncing up and down, pounding my fist on the arm of the couch, yelling, "That's not what I said! … Okay, it's what I said … but it's not *everything* I said!"

For starters, everyone on the show kept calling the Bowen Building "the Peoria Asylum", giving the impression that the Bowen was the only building of the hospital, and completely ignoring the other twelve remaining buildings.

As if that wasn't bad enough, all the investigators kept banging on about electroshock therapy. "Come on out, it's time for your electroshock therapy!" The Bowen was the nurses' dormitory and classrooms. It was even referred to, when the asylum was open, as the Employee's Building. Trying to get spirits riled up by mentioning unpleasant medical treatments in the Bowen Building is as dumb as being at a college and investigating in the biology lab looking for an athlete who died playing a game of basketball in the gym.

Britt and KJ tried their best to debunk the nurse picture that was taken several years ago, which appears to show a nurse, her hair up in a graceful Gibson-girl bun, standing at a second-floor window. They concluded that the picture was genuine (although they kept theorizing that it was the White Lady, rather than, you know, a nurse. In a white uniform. In the nurses' dorm.).

I know these guys come in cold, knowing very little of the history of the places they investigate. And I truly think they were led to believe that the Bowen was the sum total of the asylum. But for heaven's sake, make an effort. If these investigators had bothered to do *any* research, they could have asked better questions. They could have gotten better results. And isn't that why we do this? To communicate?

Two investigators put a meter directly on top of a strap, which they were told was "an actual restraint, used on a patient to tie them up". They got no response on the meter whatsoever. And why should they? Restraints were never, ever used at the asylum. Dr. Zeller saw to that. The "restraints" got no more notice from the spirits than would, say, a stapler. And if the TAPS team had done even a little research, they'd have realized that if someone had handed them a strap and told them that it was a restraint used at the Peoria State Hospital, then that artifact was a complete fake.

Things were not much better in Cemetery Two (which the investigators referred to as "the cemetery", again ignoring the other graveyards). Britt and KJ were wandering around *trying to find Bookbinder's tree.* You know—the tree that died soon after Bookbinder did. In 1910. Over a hundred years ago. When KJ slapped the trunk of a tree and declared, "This has gotta be it," I just slid down in my seat, covered my eyes, and groaned. To be fair, I told them Bookbinder's story when they interviewed me on Friday, and they were investigating at nearly 3 am Thursday morning. So maybe they had forgotten that the tree dying was an integral part of Old Book's story.

I will admit (because I get asked about this more often than anything else in regards to that episode) that I was intrigued by the shadowy figure the thermal imaging camera caught at the tree line at the edge of Cemetery Two. Yes, it was outside, so yes, you have to be awfully concerned about contamination ... but when they tried to replicate it, there was a noticeable difference between that figure and the camera guys tromping through the woods. The camera has a function where if it detects movement, it puts little boxes around the motion. When the investigators sent guys to walk around in the tree line, the camera's screen filled up with those little boxes. There's no motion box around the figure. Add in the fact that the figure just sort of appeared in the middle of the tree line—it didn't walk onto the screen from the left side and then cross to the right—and I think you've got some fairly intriguing evidence. (We'll take a much closer look at that shadowy figure when we get to the chapter on "Mysterious Deaths and Murders". Stay tuned!)

So! Yes, I got to be on an episode of Ghost Hunters. And it's kind of cool when people come up to me at work and say, "Hey, I saw you on TV last night!", I'm not gonna lie. But if you watch the episode, just take it with a grain or ten of salt. Or a whole fistful. Me, I just shake my head and say, "History, guys. Do your research."

OTHER PARANORMAL GROUPS

Scott Gaddis and his paranormal investigation team, Ghost Duck, had an extraordinary experience in the basement of the Bowen Building. They've visited the building five times, and got great results—enough to keep them coming back for more. But their encounter on January 3, 2016, was one they will never forget.

The team was down in the basement, in the farthest room on the Pfeiffer Road end of the building, in the room fancifully known as "the chapel". (There had been a chapel on the first floor, and the staff of the Bowen moved the door to that room to serve as the door to the basement room.) The team asked if any spirits were around, and immediately both the KII meter and the Rempod lit up with a positive response. The team tried to debunk this, making sure it wasn't one of their cell phones setting off the meter. Just to be safe, they had all put their phones on airplane mode. When airplane mode is off, and a KII meter swings close to the phone, the meter will flash its lights in a steady pulse. One of the investigators turned airplane mode off and demonstrated this for the camera. He was right—the pulsing looked nothing like the glowing "positive" response from the meter the group had gotten just moments earlier.

Scott reminded the group that they only had about ten minutes before they had to pack up and head home for the night. He said, "You wanna try upstairs one more time? I haven't been up to the second floor yet." The ghost hunters heard nothing in the room at the time. But someone had something to contribute.

When Scott reviewed the tape, a girl's voice said, loud and crystal clear, *"You better get upstairs quick then!"* 👻

Addison Blair and Jeff Luczkowiak are enthusiastic ghost hunters who are very passionate about what they do. Jeff's aunt gave him a brick from the Bowen Building, and the guys decided to do a quick investigation of the brick. Objects can also hold energy, so sometimes it's not necessary to go out to a site— sometimes the site comes to you. Sort of.

Jeff decided to do what we call a "flashlight session" with the brick. This is where you put a flashlight down, with its base ever so gently unscrewed. The idea is that the spirits can make contact using the flashlight; it's set so that the most delicate touch will turn it on. You ask questions, and the theory is that the spirits will turn the light on for yes, and turn it off for no.

Jeff set the brick on a bookshelf, then set the flashlight very carefully down on the brick, in the off position. Addison, just for his own peace of mind, began to read the Twenty-Third Psalm ("The Lord is my shepherd..."). He told me that he usually does this at investigations as a matter of principle. He didn't feel that there was anything malicious or evil about the brick in any way.

Jeff backed away from the brick and the flashlight, and Addison began to read. He got as far as "He restores my soul", and the flashlight, which had been off, turned on—and jumped forward a couple of inches. It stayed on as Addison finished the psalm. 👻

Shane Cleer, of Central Illinois Ghost Hunters, used to volunteer at the Bowen Building. He tells me that once, at an event, he saw a blue orb the size of a golf ball streak across the lawn.

He also shared this story with me: he and a buddy of his, Jason, were standing at the side door of the building (on Constitution Drive, on the opposite side from Pfeiffer Road). Shane was standing with his back to the door, which was locked. This was before the asbestos in the building had been abated, so no one was allowed inside anyway. Shane was wearing a hoodie, and he says that as he and Jason talked, something grabbed his hood and yanked him firmly backward.

On another visit, Shane and a friend were doing some recording at a basement window at the back of the building. Again, this was when the Bowen was locked up tight, with no one allowed inside because of the asbestos. The recorder caught sounds from inside the building, sounds that only came through on the recorder.

"It sounded as though the building was still in operation. We could hear squeaky wheelchairs and things being moved."

Another CIGH member, Dawn Kelch, shared a story that happened back in the days of urban exploration. "I was in high school, so this was in 1989. Five of us girls wanted to explore the Bowen. We were walking around, and there was just debris everywhere." As they wandered the halls, the girls heard a faint sound. "We all thought it was a cat—that's what it sounded like at first." But as they got farther down the hall, the sound got louder ... and decidedly less cat-like.

"It was a full-blown baby screaming," Dawn told me.

Remember what I said earlier, about knowing the history of a place? How if you know the history, any paranormal experience you may have might make a lot more sense? There actually is a reason the sound of a baby's cries might be picked up in the hallways of the Bowen. The Employees' Building, as it was known in the early days, was one of the first large edifices to be built. The asylum accepted its first patients in February 1902. The influx of patients soon overran the available beds in the A and B Row cottages, so places had to be found for the new patients to stay while cottages were being built on C Row. Male patients slept in the storehouse, while female patients were housed with the nurses in the Employees' Building. They stayed there for a brief period, less than a year, while the cottages were being finished.

Dawn and her friends may have been interested to know that there were children born at the asylum in the very early days. Many early patients came from poorhouses, where men and women were rarely separated, and almost never supervised. Some female patients arrived at the asylum pregnant, and gave birth there. Children were cherished, and Dr. Zeller decided that children should remain with their mothers until the age of four. So the squalling that Dawn and her friends heard could well have been a very early, very young resident of the building.

Another bit of paranormal evidence we have for the children of the Peoria State Hospital is a picture taken by an investigator named Tonya, who has done a lot of ghost hunting at the Bowen. She captured a little ghost girl near the tree line in the field across from the Bowen. The girl stands with her back to the camera. It looks like her long hair is in pigtails, with the braids falling over the front of her shoulders. She seems to be dressed in a girl's outfit from the 1920s, a short dress with tall knee socks (although her legs are indistinct).

This picture is interesting in itself, but it's even more interesting when you place it in the context of history. Children actually did play in the field where that picture was taken! The Industrial Building used to stand across the street from the Bowen, and there was a field that separated it from the woods. Employees were allowed to bring their children to work with them, and some of the patients at the asylum were children. There was no "us" and "them" at the asylum. Because so many of the patients had tasks to do, to help keep the asylum running, the person you worked with every day was most likely a patient. These kids played together all over the hilltop. Tonya seems to have captured one of these little ones—whether she was a patient or the daughter of an employee, we don't know. But she's still out there playing in the field.

Are there other children playing with her?

This little ghost girl caught on film may have been a patient, or the child of an employee. We'll never know.

James Barrow is a huge fan of the Peoria State Hospital, and he has made many trips through the Bowen. Some of the spirits there even seem to recognize him, and this makes for some really wonderful EVPs.

In the spring of 2015, James caught some interesting audio evidence using a Sony digital voice recorder and an RT-EVP device, which lets you listen to EVPs in "real time" (hence the RT part of the name). James visited the Bowen on March 15, 2015 to celebrate his birthday with a ghost hunt. He ended up getting a wonderful birthday present from the spirits. Up in one of the tower rooms in the attic, the group caught an EVP right after the guide said, "This is where they kept the files for the patients." A female voice corrected, *"This is my room."* Soon after that, someone threw a plastic Easter egg at the group.

That's a heck of a birthday present for any ghost hunter.

The next month's visit, on June 16, 2015, yielded a wealth of spirit box communication. James was there with an investigator named Jerry Zilch, a guide at the Bowen and member of Spirits in the Night. Together, they had some illuminating conversation with the ghosts of the Bowen.

At one point, James and Jerry are throwing out names, trying to connect with known inhabitants of the Bowen. Jerry asks, "Are you Mrs. Zeller?"

A voice from the spirit box confirms, *"Sophie."*

If you listen to this, and I hope you do, please remember that during a spirit box session, the spirits use the snippets of sound to form words. You are not hearing what their voice actually sounded like. In theory, you are hearing whatever sound they can pick up on the radio band that corresponds to what they want to convey. It's an imprecise science, is what I'm trying to say. Keep that in mind when you read this next bit, too.

It seems that Rhoda Derry took the opportunity to introduce herself to Jerry. The two men were in the attic of the Bowen, when over the spirit box, a strangely accented, almost mincing voice came through.

"So nice to meet you. The name is Rhoda."

James confirmed for me that this was one of the first spirit box communications he got from a spirit that may be Rhoda Derry. Maybe she was still trying to suss out how to speak using this weird device. I don't have all the answers, I just have an open mind, a sense of wonder, and a whole lot of faith.

The evening's excitement continued, with the spirit box providing a running commentary. On the third floor, James noted his location and the date for the recorder. The spirit box assured him, *"We're right with you."* Soon after that, a ghost took advantage of the spirit box to give its opinion of the group of investigators.

"They ain't doctors."

One of the most charming EVPs to come out of that evening was a voice caught in the basement. James had brought a small stuffed cow as a gift for "Sarah", one of the child spirits who called the Bowen home. Just like a child, it seems that "Sarah" had to be prompted a bit. James set the toy down, then said,

"Can I have a thank you for it?"

The spirit box shyly, softly said *"Thank you."*

A few days later, James came to the Bowen again (June 26, 2015). One of the female investigators tried to speak with "Sarah", asking if there was anything she had to say.

"Give us ... more toys," a boy's voice responded over the spirit box.

The Bowen Building was the scene of many fascinating experiences and forms the backdrop to the memories of many area residents. When people went to visit their relatives at the asylum, those family reunions took place on the wide, welcoming lawn of the Bowen, with the comforting stone bulk of the building rising behind them. And when the asylum began its new life as a haunted hotspot, many investigators—and many other people—had paranormal encounters in and around the building. It was a monument to compassionate care, and it was a rich source of paranormal activity. It was definitely a place worth visiting.

I'm sorry to say, though, that you cannot visit the Bowen. No one can. That's because the Bowen no longer exists. It was torn down over the long, painful summer of 2017. The last occupants of the Bowen Building wrung every last dime they could out of her old bones. Then, when the paranormal tours dried up, when the building had outlived her usefulness to them, they tore her down, claiming they wanted to salvage the limestone. As this book goes to press, none of the nearly $1 million the occupants borrowed from the city of Bartonville has been paid back. None of it.

The Bowen Building is gone. The lovely pine floorboards that Dr. Zeller paced while teaching student nurses are now tossed in a jumbled pile in someone's back yard, awaiting their turn in the bonfire. There's only an empty field where George and Sophie Zeller's last home once stood. Not even a crumb of limestone marks the grand old building where young nurses were trained in the compassionate care of the mentally ill.

But the Bowen has joined the ranks of the ghosts that inhabit the hilltop. The memories last ... and so do the stories.

THE FIREHOUSE

Firehouse Image

The firehouse as it appeared in the early days of the asylum

At the height of the asylum's expansion, there were sixty-three buildings on the hilltop. With the loss of the Bowen, only twelve of those buildings remain.

Happily, one of those buildings is the firehouse. This was one of the earliest structures put up on the hilltop, and it served several purposes. It was built in 1889, and its first use was as a barn for pigs and horses. The horses were hitched to wagons which picked up building supplies at the train station and shuttled them to the various building sites. The powerhouse, the general storehouse, and even the ill-fated Kirkbride building were built with the help of these sturdy beasts. The barn's hayloft provided sleeping quarters for workmen and possibly some male patients in the very early days.

The state hospital was such a desperately needed institution that patients began to arrive as soon as it opened. There was room for seven hundred patients in the A and B Row cottages. These were soon filled to capacity, and still, patients in need of care continued to arrive. The general storehouse actually served as temporary housing for the overflow of male patients, just as the extra female patients were put up in the Employees' Building. Up to one hundred-fifty male patients called the general storehouse home until their cottages were finished.

After the asylum was up and running, the horses and wagons were still used for hauling goods around the hilltop. But they soon had other duties—the horses pulled the wagons for the fire brigade. In early 1930, a second story and attic were added to the horse barn, and it became a full-fledged firehouse, with the firemen sleeping in the upper part of the building. It continued in this capacity until 1973. (For those interested, after the asylum closed in 1973, boxes of paperwork were stored in the building. It was used as a private home for a while, then it was rented to a succession of businesses before becoming the Peoria State Hospital Museum.)

Now, after a life of service, the building has been given a new use, one just as important as housing workmen or sheltering fire equipment. It now serves as the home of the Peoria State Hospital Museum. It's so fitting that the museum is in the earliest structure to be built on the hilltop.

The museum is a treasure house of artifacts from the asylum's storied history. The museum's collection of hundreds of newspaper clippings is invaluable to researchers interested in getting a first-hand look at the asylum's past.

Christina Morris, the historian of Peoria State Hospital and curator of the museum, reigns over a constantly changing array of artifacts. "We have so many items, we just can't put them all out at once," she says. So she presides over a rotating display of items connected with the hospital's history.

These artifacts come from all over central Illinois. Some have been donated to the museum by former staff members. One of the permanent displays is a large shallow metal tray, about seven feet long, standing innocuously in the corner of one of the rooms. Those of you who may be faint of heart may want to skip the rest of this sentence ... this tray was known as a death sled, and yes, it was used at the Zeller Hospital to transport deceased patients. When the asylum closed, many of the staff members were allowed to take some of the equipment home. An employee who worked at Zeller Hospital from 1959 to 1973 decided that a sturdy metal death sled would make the perfect tray on which to display ... potted plants. This death sled saw decades of use even after the asylum closed, celebrating life and green growing things, until the employee donated it a few years ago. This former employee had come to the Pollak Hospital and the museum for a tour. She was so impressed with the job Christina Morris was doing to keep the history of the asylum alive, that she donated the death sled directly to Christina, who then added it to the museum collection.

One of the smaller rooms of the museum is set up to resemble a nurses' dorm room, in a nod to the vanished Bowen Building. Dr. Zeller, always in search of the most efficient way to run his asylum, realized that one bed could be made to serve the sleeping needs of two student nurses. Kind of like the bunk arrangements on a submarine, one nurse would use the bed at night, and a nurse who happened to have a night shift would sleep during the day. A room was $8 a month, unless you shared. Then the cost went up to $12, but split between two girls, the cost to each student nurse was only $6 a month. Enrollment in the Peoria State Hospital's top-shelf nursing program, especially in the first decades of the century, was so high anyway that this rotating use of the beds really made sense. This bed-sharing only affected the student nurses. After graduation, nurses either moved into one of the staff cottages on the grounds or found housing in Bartonville.

Another permanent display in the museum is the only surviving Utica crib from the asylum's early days, and its travels make for a fascinating story. Those familiar with the story of

Rhoda Derry will know exactly what a Utica crib is, and those familiar with the early history of the Peoria State Hospital will know exactly why it's such a miracle that this piece of furniture has survived all these years. Let me explain.

One of Dr. Zeller's most dearly-held principles was his belief in absolute non-restraint. He utterly forbade the use of any kind of restraint at his asylum—no straitjackets, no handcuffs, no foot shackles, no bed saddles, and no Utica cribs. When the asylum was built, it was furnished with the standard equipment found in mental hospitals of the day, which meant bars on the windows, a supply of restraints, and a couple of Utica cribs. (A Utica crib is exactly what it sounds like: it looks like a baby's crib, except that it sits low to the floor, and it has a barred lid—which locks.)

One of Dr. Zeller's first acts when he took charge as superintendent was to remove all the bars from the windows. Of course, since the facility was a state hospital, he then had to account for his decision. (Basically, the state said, "You've just removed $6,000 worth of hardware from the windows of your institution. What do you propose to do with all of it?") Dr. Zeller repurposed the window grilles into cages for a petting zoo on the grounds. The Utica cribs became rabbit hutches, or were used as mangers to hold hay for the deer.

Dr. Zeller kept just one of the Utica cribs out of the zoo enclosure, and here's where it gets interesting. He would fill the crib with all of the straitjackets and handcuffs—the familiar trappings of insanity—and he would take it around to state fairs and other social gatherings. He would put all these reminders of mental illness on display, simply to be able to reassure people that if they were to send a relative to the Peoria State Hospital, their loved one would never be subjected to the use of these barbaric relics. And that is the only reason why one of the Utica cribs survived until the asylum's closing.

When Rhoda Derry arrived at the asylum on September 26, 1904, Dr. Zeller convinced the Adams County Almshouse to also send him the box bed and Utica crib in which Rhoda had spent the past forty-four years. (For Rhoda's complete story, please see my book *44 Years in Darkness*.) Dr. Zeller put these items in his collection as yet another example of the barbaric treatment that would not be tolerated at his institution. Some of these items, as well as the restraints, were eventually moved to the Zeller Museum at the Zeller Zone Center in Peoria, and some were sent to Bradley University.

When the asylum closed in December 1973, some of the equipment was packed up and sent off to the museum at the SIU School of Medicine in Carbondale, Illinois. This included the items at the Zeller Museum. They were part of the SIU collection until a few years ago, when I tracked them down with help from Arlene Parr. (Arlene helped write *Bittersweet Memories*, a collection of reminiscences about the hospital.) I called the museum at SIU and asked very politely if we could please have our Utica crib back. They agreed. A couple of Peoria State Museum staff members drove down to Carbondale and retrieved the Utica crib and other asylum artifacts, including restraints, some paintings, and a gray wool blanket. To the intense delight of the museum personnel, the blanket had a handwritten exhibit tag attached, which turned out to be in Dr. Zeller's handwriting.

Unfortunately, Rhoda's crib and box bed were not among the artifacts retrieved from SIU. They are still somewhere in the museum system—we're not exactly sure where they are. Curators at the Peoria State Hospital Museum are still working on tracking them down, so we can bring them home as well.

With all the artifacts in the building, and all the history swirling around, it's no wonder that the museum is haunted to the rafters. The building comes alive with various bumps in the night—most of the activity in the museum comes in the form of unexplainable thumps and knocks.

When I was working on writing *44 Years in Darkness*, I went to the museum to consult with Christina Morris, the resident expert on all things historical at the asylum. We were supposed to meet at the museum at one in the afternoon, and I got there a little early. I didn't see her truck in the parking lot, but just to be safe, I got out of my car and knocked on the door to the museum. There's a staircase that leads to the second floor, and it starts right next to the front door, in the foyer. I clearly heard footsteps coming down that staircase, so I said to myself, "Oh good, Christina's here after all." Long moments went by, while I waited for her to open the door. I frowned, and cupped my hands to peer in the display window. I saw no movement inside at all. The room was dark, and no one had come to unlock the door. I pulled out my phone and texted Christina.

You're not at the museum yet, are you?

Nope. Got caught up in another errand. Sorry—be there soon.

I shook my head, grinning. The spirits of the asylum—well, one spirit in particular—had skunked me.

One of the volunteers, Dustin, spent quite some time volunteering at the firehouse. This gave him plenty of opportunities to witness the personality of the building.

"One time I was cleaning, and I watched a door just start to sway back and forth." He has also heard giggling in the attic. "It was two different girl laughs. I kinda think they were playing up there."

The nights, in particular, are busy with paranormal activity. One night, Dustin was working late at the museum, and was falling asleep in spite of himself. He had just dropped off when he heard four hard knocks on the front door, bangs hard enough to jangle the sleigh bells attached to the door.

"I woke up, still half asleep, and said, 'Guys, someone's at the front door.' Then I said to myself, 'Shit, I'm alone.' So I went downstairs and opened the door. No one was there." The phantom door banging repeated itself a few days later. This time, there were three other witnesses there with Dustin.

Other than that, the museum seems to be the scene of a fairly garden-variety haunting ... footsteps downstairs when you know you're the only one in the building, small objects moved from place to place, things like that.

Draven, another museum volunteer, often gets tapped to carry stuff up to the building's attic. It's pretty obvious when someone is moving around in the attic; footsteps on the attic floor are very distinctive, and noticeable to anyone on the second floor. Many times, museum volunteers hear footsteps in the attic, and assume it's Draven shuffling around up there. And then Draven comes into the room where everyone is gathered … and the footsteps are still going on overhead.

This particular phenomenon is actually helpful to historians. You didn't think that footsteps could date a haunting, did you? It's true. We know that the firehouse didn't have an attic until a renovation in early 1930. Therefore, if someone invisible is stomping around up there, odds are their spirit arrived around that time.

Christina Morris, the curator of the museum, has a theory on who haunts the firehouse. There was a patient at the asylum in the early days whose mania manifested in setting fires and watching them burn—in short, he was a pyromaniac. No one quite realized this at first. As with all able-bodied patients, this fellow was required to work at the asylum. He expressed an interest in helping with the fire brigade, and secretly (for a while) indulged his passion for the flames.

A bit of explanation is in order here: there's a big difference between a modern fire truck and the "fire brigade" of the early twentieth century. The early fire trucks weren't tankers or pumpers; they carried buckets. In case of fire, the trucks raced to the nearest water source, and patients and staff literally formed a bucket brigade. Bodies of water were scattered around the grounds for exactly this reason—including the pond in front of the Bowen Building.

So for a while, the firebug was able to satisfy his compulsion to watch the dancing flames. For a while … until he was discovered actually setting fires to get his fix. The final straw came when he threw a dog onto a crackling bonfire. The dog was dead, but that was the end of the fellow's career in the asylum fire brigade.

This patient seems to have been a bit simple, as well as mentally ill. His behavior seems to be that of a trickster—he's pushed people on the stairs, and he likes to jangle the bells at the door. He also likes to turn on televisions and radios.

One of the volunteers—Weapons is his nickname—was sitting in the firehouse in one of the second floor rooms with a few other museum folks. There was a huge television set, the old kind that's built into a cabinet, in the corner of the room.

Weapons was sitting on one side of the TV set, and Draven was one the other side.

As they sat talking, Weapons heard a high-pitched whine. He has bad hearing, so he assumed it was just his ears playing tricks on him. But Draven glanced over at him with a curious look.

"Did you hear that?"

Just then, the TV turned itself on. Frowning, Weapons snapped it off. And it turned back on again.

Now, you may be thinking, well, old television sets are glitchy. Maybe the wiring was wonky, and it just ... turned itself on somehow. But modern radios in the building, including a radio with an iPhone deck, have also switched themselves on and started blasting out music.

(That, incidentally, is why the museum staff won't keep heaters in the second floor rooms. It's one thing to have a radio randomly spill music out into the air. To have the electronic ignition on a space heater spontaneously turn itself on ... well, that's just dangerous.)

Of course, putting the trickster spirit aside, there's another very good reason that the museum is exceedingly haunted. The shelves and cases in the small building are crammed with personal artifacts, reminders that the patients who lived here were real people, not just names in newspaper articles or numbers on gravestones. Here's a jar that once held cold cream. Here's a tube of long-vanished lipstick. Here's a mirror, yet more proof of the simple pleasure a patient took in being pampered. The instructions for nurses included things like "make sure every patient gets their hands and face washed and their hair combed every day". Little things like that went a long way towards reminding the mentally ill of their personal worth.

Jars of buttons line the shelves. Simple things, bits of daily life. Pieces of broken crockery found in the four garbage dump sites for the asylum remind us that people drank coffee in the morning, just as we do. A pair of wire eyeglass frames sits near the porcelain face of a doll, a doll that was once cuddled by a child.

One of the coolest small artifacts in the museum is a

strange-looking gadget, a metal tube on top of a chunky black base with a dodgy-looking cord coming out of it. An hour and a half of research on the patent number inscribed on the base revealed the answer to the mystery: it's a curling iron. The patent for the device was issued in 1925. You put the curling iron into the tube, which heated up, and heated the iron. The handles of the actual curling iron part are taped, the original melamine having cracked off long ago.

The museum proudly displays Dr. Zeller's china cabinet, the death sled, a chair from one of the dining halls, the one surviving Utica crib from the early days. But these smaller items, the articles of daily life, the thimbles, the saucers, the hairbrushes … these are the things that speak of everyday moments, caught in time.

These are the things that attract the spirits.

Artifacts at the Peoria State Hospital Museum.
The death sled is propped up in the corner.

A student nurse's bed, shared in shifts.

THE POLLAK HOSPITAL

By 1906, tuberculosis—the "white death"—had become the leading cause of death at Peoria State Hospital. Between June 30, 1905 and June 30, 1906, sixty-four patients were taken by the disease. Dr. Zeller realized that something had to be done to stop the spread of this insidious threat. He wisely decided to quarantine those suffering from tuberculosis in their own little area on the hilltop.

This was the beginning of the "tent colonies" at the asylum. It started off by using the porch of one of the newer cottages. Dr. Zeller ordered heavy canvas sheets to be installed on the porch, to be rolled up in good weather, and rolled down and secured to form temporary walls in cold weather. (In really viciously cold weather, the patients were taken inside.)

Six patients spent the entire winter of 1905 in this first tent arrangement. Dr. Zeller was delighted with the results. These happened to be six of the most acute patients, and Dr. Zeller reported that "a number of them are still alive to testify to the efficacy of the outdoor experiment." Unfortunately, his report didn't specify how many of the six did actually make it through the winter.

Inspired by this success, Dr. Zeller decided to set up a proper tent colony. The arrangement consisted of one big wall tent (18' x 24'), with smaller (9' x 9') tents off of the main tent. The largest tent was heated with a wood stove, and as at the cottages, the walls were rolled up to let fresh air in during good weather, and tacked down when the weather turned bad. This was another huge success, with sixteen women and ten men treated in the tents through the winter of 1906.

Dr. Zeller also had solariums set up on the hilltop. These buildings were quite beautiful, as well as being dedicated to the care of consumptive patients. A two-story building rose in the center, with ruby-colored glass windows from ground to ceiling. Dr. Zeller believed that colored light was beneficial to restore health to tubercular patients, so they were bathed in red light, sunlight turned to jewel tones through the windows. Six one-story tents were clustered at the base, three on each side. The tents were 30' by 30', about the size of a large room.

Open-air therapy in the tent colony worked wonders for the consumptive patients. In a bid to improve treatment even more, Dr. Zeller decided to separate tuberculosis patients from the rest of the population entirely. He had a batwing-shaped hospital built on the same land as one of the original tent colonies. This building, which housed patients as early as 1913, was replaced in 1949 by the Pollak Hospital. The Pollak actually shares part of its footprint with the batwing hospital, in the Pollak Women's Ward.

The Pollak is unique in that it is the only remaining asylum building on the hilltop that is dedicated to paranormal research. It is managed by Doom Industries. This is the business that constructs and runs the Haunted Infirmary every October. The rest of the year, the building is the scene of paranormal and historical tours. Ghost research groups clamor to investigate the Pollak.

The Pollak is an incredibly rich source of paranormal experiences. Imagine putting a floor plan of the Pollak down on a big table. Now picture laying a sheet of transparent plastic over it, like the sheets teachers used to use for overhead projectors. Make marks, maybe little "x"s, on that sheet with a blue pen, for visual sightings of apparitions. Now take another sheet and lay it on top, and mark audio phenomena in red pen. Do the same thing with another sheet of plastic and a yellow pen for the phantom smells people have experienced in different parts of the building. Use an orange pen for when people have been touched. Maybe choose a green pen to mark where EVPs have been recorded. Use a purple pen to note just random weirdness. When you're finished, you're going to have a rainbow of "x"s all over the building's footprint. Supernatural phenomena happen in every single part of this building, and what happens involves every one of the senses—every single one, including, for some, the sixth sense.

I don't know if it's because the building is constantly being used for research except for the months of August through October, when the haunt is built and presented. Maybe the spirits congregate there because of all the investigative and haunt activity. Or maybe it's because people are actively searching for paranormal evidence there, and occurrences in other asylum buildings go unreported (but not unnoticed). Whatever the reason, the Pollak fairly hums with spectral activity.

The spirits at the Pollak are so eager to communicate that quite often, they don't even wait for the ghost hunting to start before making their presence known. A Pollak tour always starts out with a historical slide show, outlining the history of the asylum. You can't fully understand the hauntings of a place without knowing the history behind the ghost stories. The slide show includes pictures of the asylum as it looked back in the early days, and in its prime. Historical photos of the cottages decorated for patients' birthdays give viewers an idea of the care the staff took to meet the social needs of the patients, and to create an atmosphere of home.

Diane Lockhart, a psychic medium, has been to the Pollak several times. She has a distinct advantage on investigations—she can see spirits, and hear them. (She sees the spirits as solid figures, just not as solid as a living person.) On one tour Diane attended, she was sitting in the Men's Ward, where the slide show was presented. She saw a female spirit sitting near another (living) lady. The ghost looked around, noticed Diane noticing her, and chirped, *"I lived there"*, nodding to the screen where a picture of a cottage was displayed.

"She said it like it was a happy memory," Diane says. "She looked at me and talked directly to me." The historical slide show is an integral, non-negotiable part of a Pollak tour. It's no wonder that a spirit in search of a dose of happy nostalgia would choose to sit in on a presentation.

I had my own personal experience with spirits who just

couldn't wait for that night's investigation to start. One Saturday evening in March, I arrived at the Pollak to play my part in the kitchen scene, the re-creation of the incident in which a dietician was attacked and killed by a patient. (You can read this story in a later chapter, "Mysterious Deaths and Murders".) It had been a long day, and for me, the day wasn't over yet. I wasn't feeling particularly sociable, so after getting into costume, instead of hanging out with the other actors at the front entrance of the building, I headed by myself down to the Women's Ward to get on scene.

I had brought a book with me, so I grabbed a handy milk crate, turned it over for a seat, and sat down to pass the time. I had been reading for a short while, about ten minutes or so, when all of a sudden, the lights went out.

I honestly didn't connect it with anything supernatural at the time. I just thought it was odd that we'd gone "lights out" for the investigation, but we hadn't done the tour of the building yet. I raised my voice and said, "Hey, I'm actually back here in the kitchen. I'm reading a book, so, um, could you turn the lights back on please?"

The lights promptly came back on, and I settled back down with my book. I thought very briefly that it was also odd that I hadn't gotten a response to my shouted request to turn the lights back on. No one had hollered back, "Oh, sorry, we didn't know anyone was back here!" (Of course, no one giggled loudly and said "Gotcha!" either, so I figured it wasn't some other volunteer pranking me.) The lights just came back on, that's all.

I sat there reading for about ten more minutes. The milk crate wasn't the most comfortable seat, but I was enjoying the book. (Here's a bit of synchronicity for you: I was reading *Asylum Light*, by James Sheridan Ward, one of the histories of the Peoria State Hospital. I swear I'm not making this up.)

As I sat there reading about Dr. Zeller and the glory days of the asylum, I heard a noise from the corner of the kitchen, right at the door Evan and I would both barge through when we did the scene. The door was within six feet of me, so I heard the sound very clearly.

It was a rather exasperated sigh.

I have no idea who made the noise. I could just picture a spirit standing there watching me, impatient to get the show on the road. Or maybe it was a sigh of confusion. Here's a living woman, sitting all alone in the Women's Ward, but she's not asking questions, she doesn't have any equipment, she's just sitting there with her nose stuck in a book. What's up with that?

After the tour, when the investigation was well under way, I found Christina Morris and told her about the lights being turned off on me, and then coming back on when I pointed out I was actually in the area trying to read. She laughed, and told me that spirits playing with the lights is a pretty common occurrence in the Women's Ward.

"We'll be leaving the building late at night, we'll go through and turn off every single light, we'll lock the building and go out to our cars—and there'll be lights on in the Women's Ward."

By far the best bit of weirdness that has shown up even before an investigation starts is the utterly odd, perfectly delightful anomaly we've dubbed "the Thingie".

Paranormal investigations at the Pollak Hospital follow a predictable pattern. Investigators gather in the Peoria State Hospital Museum, just a couple of blocks away from the Pollak, for two slide shows, the first on the history of the Peoria State Hospital, and the second showing some of the paranormal evidence we've collected over the years. Christina Morris, the historian of the Peoria State Hospital, narrates both shows. Then she'll take the group on a walkthrough of the Pollak Building, pointing out the hot spots. Then it's off to the Men's Ward, where Christina goes over what investigators can expect to encounter over the course of the evening. Sometimes, at this point, she'll toss in a bit more history. This last pep talk before the ghost hunters get down to business always includes a discussion of the basement. The walkthrough includes the basement, but it's the last stop before returning to the Men's Ward for final instructions. The group has had to assimilate quite a lot of information by that point, so Christina gives them some pointers, many of which are particularly relevant to investigating in the basement.

This was a private tour—it was Dale Kaczmarek's group

Ghost Research Society—so Christina knew that this bunch of seasoned investigators would benefit from a little less ghost hunting advice and a little more of the building's history. It's always good to know the history of the place you're investigating, to be better able to tailor the questions you ask. You're liable to get better responses that way.

Christina was describing the basement's use as a cold storage facility. The slab that forms the floor of the Pollak basement was actually poured over a natural spring, one of the springs that honeycomb the hilltop. There's a theory in paranormal circles that the ionizing effects of running water tend to attract supernatural energy. This means that the basement of the Pollak is the most active place in one of the most active buildings on the grounds. The workmen who built the Pollak weren't thinking about the fact that the spring would be a dandy source of paranormal energy. They were thinking much more practically: the spring water under the concrete would help to keep the basement nice and cool, even during the heat of the summer months. In short, the basement was an excellent place to temporarily store the bodies of the unfortunate patients who passed away upstairs.

There are 4,132 graves in the three cemeteries on the hilltop, but those graves represent only about a quarter of the patients whose lives ended here. Most patients were sent home to be buried in family plots. Their bodies were wrapped tightly in white sheets, and taken down to the coolness of the basement to await being placed on a train for the final ride home.

Christina was standing on a low stage at the front of the Men's Ward, describing this to the group. To her right was a nearly solid wall of lumber and boxes, about as tall as her shoulders. As Christina spoke about the bodies being wrapped in sheets before being sent home, a white shape popped up from the area to her right. It looked like a wad of white fabric, a slim shape that hung in the air for several long moments, looking for all the world like a faceless sock puppet. Christina continued to talk—her peripheral vision registered the anomaly, but being a professional speaker, she finished what she was saying before giving in to curiosity.

And the people watching the talk certainly noticed. As Christina spoke, there were murmurs, soft at first, then growing louder. "What *is* that?" The oddity held still for a few more seconds, then it hunch-skittered away towards the back of the stage. Christina looked to her right, but the Thingie had already scuttled off. People stammered an explanation of the bizarre little sock puppet they'd seen. A grin spread across Christina's face as she listened to the brabble of excitement. "Maybe we caught it on camera, that'd be great!"

(Fortunately for all of us, the camera *did* capture the Thingie. Stan Suho was taping at the time, and Kathie Para was the first to notice the anomaly. You can see the video clip on the Ghost Research Society website.)

THE HAUNTED INFIRMARY

The Haunted Infirmary is a staple of the Halloween season in central Illinois. In an area full of weekend scares, the "Haunt" is consistently a fan favorite. Christina Morris, in her alter ego as "The Mistress", presides over the haunt, keeping it running smoothly and riding herd on the many actors. The energy stirred up by hundreds of visitors over the weekends of October really brings out the spirits of the Pollak, and if you're lucky enough to go on a ghost hunt during November, the activity is off the charts as a result. And it starts in October. There have been plenty of haunt volunteers who've had paranormal encounters in the halls and rooms of the Pollak.

Kristin Vogel tells one such story. "It was the start of the final weekend of the Infirmary, 2016. I was going over the final details of my scene as the hall lights went out, signaling that the first group would be coming soon. Everyone began scurrying back to their scenes excited to start the night. I distinctly remember there being a strong positive energy among everyone as we waited for Christina to start the C-Ward callout.

"As I approached my doorway and took in the mixed murmur of the haunt ambiance, I was interrupted by a man behind me saying, quite nonchalantly, 'Hey, turn around.' Naturally, I spun around expecting to see Tal, Draven, or Jeff. There was no one there and I instantly froze in place and raised my hands up as a reflex. I tried to rapidly analyze and rationalize the situation. I quickly also remembered that the scenes before *and* after mine were empty. Nobody was close enough to have spoken at that volume and distance. It sounded like they were just a few feet behind me, as if they had walked up and said it.

"As everyone was chanting 'C WARD!' I jumped out of my scene and into the next to find Tal and scramble to explain what had just happened before the first group got sent through. I admit I was a little nervous to go back to my scene, but as I fell into character, I was able to let it slip my mind. Groups came through one after the other. To this day there has been no natural explanation, and I consider it my first paranormal experience."

One of the volunteers that's been at the haunt the longest is "Weapons" Spears. For real, that's his name. He got his nickname for his talent at making some of the gruesome props that make the Haunted Infirmary such a howling success. It's just a happy accident that his last name fits the theme as well.

Weapons is a big guy, one of those gentle giant types. And the story he told me is referred to by Christina as "the time Weapons turned into a six year old girl".

It was Weapons' first year at the haunt, which had only been in operation for two years at that time. There are two bathrooms in the foyer, directly across from each other, and that night, both bathrooms were open for the actors to fuss with their makeup. Christina, Jill, and Jackie were in the second bathroom taking their makeup off at the end of the evening, and Weapons was leaning against the wall in the hallway outside the open door. (Both bathrooms have two doors, that open into the foyer hall and into the hallway proper.)

"I figured they didn't need another body in there," Weapons told me. He had just stripped off the Tyvek suit he'd worn as a crazed patient for his haunt character, and he was standing next to a gurney that was against the wall. He'd piled the suit in a messy wad on the gurney, and set his giant can of soda next to it, leaning the can against the bunched fabric.

As Weapons slouched against the wall, he heard the indistinct murmur of a little girl's voice from one of the rooms close to the foyer. Moments later, the can of soda stood upright ("against gravity", Weapons told me), then fell over in the opposite direction.

"If I'd just heard the girl's voice, fine. If I'd just put the can down, fine—I'd have convinced myself it just fell." But both things happening at once? That was just a bit too much.

Weapons refused to be the last one out of the building for months afterward.

The door to one wing of the Men's Ward is *always* locked, no exceptions. That wing is rented out, and the renters like their privacy. Christina is happy to oblige them, no problem at all. But something inside the room has other ideas.

One October night during the haunt, in full view of several horrified haunt volunteers, the doorknob jiggled a bit ... *then the locked door swung open.*

"Get the Mistress get the Mistress get the Mistress!" someone screamed. The actors huddled together, staring at the door, until Christina arrived. Word had been passed from scene to scene that she was needed down near the Men's Ward.

"What's going on? Did someone unlock this door?" Christina demanded. *Everyone* knows that door stays locked.

"We swear, we were just watching it! We didn't touch it!"

Knowing the honesty of her volunteers—and seeing the looks on their faces—Christina believed the scared actors.

Another haunt volunteer, Cory Hill, had a role as a 1950s nurse. Her scene was close to that same door, the door of the wing across from the Men's Ward. Christina Morris, in her role as Mistress (the haunt director) would go through the haunt every evening before it opened to the public, and one of her duties was to make sure that door was locked.

Only, it didn't always *stay* locked. Cory says that on the nights she worked the haunt, she would see that door come open, as if someone had slowly turned the knob, then pushed it open. Another thing she noticed that even though the other actors in her scene would work up a sweat during the haunt from all the exertion, she always felt cold. She will admit, that freaked her out just a little. She also mentioned that as part of her scene, there was a television set that was tuned between channels, to put out just static. There was no remote to the set, but sometimes it would turn itself off without any help.

Christina has a theory: she thinks the spirits were drawn to Cory because she was dressed as a nurse from the 1950s. "I think they used to swarm her so badly because of the costume," Christina says. "She was always surrounded by people. I just didn't tell her that at the time, because I want her to come back someday!"

The Haunted Infirmary is such an elaborate production that some of the elements of the haunt stay up for a while. When you go to the Pollak for an investigation, you're quite likely to run into a bloody pile of fake guts on a cafeteria counter, or a group of sullenly brooding monks in a corner. That's all part of the haunt, of course. October has a long shelf life in the Pollak.

All these reminders of Halloween seem to stir up the spirits in the building. Maybe they remember, throughout the year, how much fun it is to have people streaming through the halls and rooms every Friday and Saturday night in October, shrieking with delighted fear in the darkness. That really pumps the spirits full of energy, much more than the quiet respect of the paranormal investigators who file in and sit in subdued silence, listening for ghost voices.

At any rate, the spirits aren't shy about creating their own scares when they can. I've found out myself that they can turn lights on and off. As I said, it didn't even register with me that a plunge into darkness had anything to do with the paranormal. But the volunteers are sometimes spooked when a light comes on by itself.

And when that light is intended to remind you of scary clowns, it's even creepier. One of the haunt rooms is—you guessed it—based on many people's bone-deep fear of clowns. It's one of the exam rooms off the hallway, an oxygen therapy room to be precise. When the light switch is pushed—and you do have to push it, it won't go off if someone just brushes up against it—a spinning ball starts up, throwing splashes of colored light all over the room and out into the hallway. Tinny music starts to play too—*deetdeet deedle-eedee deetdeet deedee*, that old familiar circus tune.

Brian, a staff member, walked into the building late one night. The building was dark, but Brian could hear faint music coming from his left. He looked down the hallway, and brightly colored light was cascading into the hallway from the oxygen therapy room, and circus music spilled its cheer into the air.

Brian was not cheered.

And the spirits learn, too. "It was one thing when they used to turn the hallway and room lights on and off. That at least makes sense, because those lights were here when they were living here. But now they've figured out *our* lights. That has become really interesting. Some of our prop lights are really creepy, they're red bulbs, they're under something, they cast weird shadows—you walk into that building in the dark, expecting darkness, and there are lights on that aren't supposed to be on … it'll creep you out," Christina says.

"Or—my favorite—you'll turn all the lights off, and you'll go into the hallway and look both ways down the hall to make sure all the lights are out. You'll look this way, then that way, then this way … and a light will be on. It was bad enough when it was just the white room lights, but now they've figured out the prop lights. So you'll be like, nothing, nothing, *spooky-ass freaking red glowy light*! I had to unplug it!

"The worst part is, you'll go all the way down the hallway in the dark, turn the light off, then start hauling ass back up the dark hallway to the front of the building. And while you're doing that, *another* light will come on, so you have to go back and turn *that* one off too. You tell me they're not doing that on purpose and getting a charge out of your fear."

Many a volunteer has balked at going down the dark hallway to turn off lights that have suddenly come back on, with no human hand on the switch. (I have to admit here that even as much as I love the Pollak and her ghosts, that would be a big "nope" moment for me too.)

"That shows intelligence, that they've learned how to turn

on our prop lights. It shows that they're smart."

"It also shows that they're smart-*asses*," AJ offered as we talked.

Christina laughed. "Right! I think they see us horsing around, playing tricks on each other, and they're mimicking us, how we interact with each other. Like the *'hey there'*s in the dark, when you know you're alone. My favorite is when we're all working on something, and I'll hear someone yell 'Hey!' I'll yell back, 'I'm down here!' and everyone will turn to look at me like, who are you talking to?"

"Or when we hear *your* voice down the hallway?" Katie reminded her. "On the opposite side of the building?"

"They'll mimic my voice," Christina told me. "They'll call the kids down the hallway, and the kids will go down that way ... and it's farther away from wherever I actually am."

The spirits like to wait until all the lights have been doused for the night, and then turn on the lights in the women's tub room, too. That, and my experience in the Women's Ward, gives us a clue as to who might be playfully cutting the lights, or turning them on after they've been turned off. At the end of the Pollak's working life, the building housed geriatric patients, including elderly women who suffered from dementia.

This playing with the lights business is trickster behavior. And locking people in the bathroom? Yeah, that happens. Tell me that's not a grade school prank. There's nothing evil going on here, the spirits aren't trying to entrap anyone. They're just trying to get a rise out of the volunteers, spooking them as they walk down the hall. These spirits have likely reverted to child-like behavior, just as they did near the end of their lives here. They've regressed, because in their minds, they see themselves as little girls. The giggling we hear in the hallways and in the Women's Ward is coming from these harmless old ladies.

Let's face it, it's just fun to scare people.

THE MEN'S WARD

The Men's Ward has always been a reliable source of paranormal experiences. Lena Haig works at the Haunted Infirmary every year, performing as the character "Monstrosity". She's been a fixture of the haunt from the very first year, and the spirits of the Pollak are familiar with her.

In the early stages of her character development, Monstrosity would crouch on the floor and snarl menacingly and expressively at people who came through the haunt. During a spirit box session one night in the basement, a ghost came through and dismissively said, "*You're ... not ... dog.*"

During one investigation, Lena and her then-boyfriend were in the Men's Ward with a couple of ghost hunters. Some energy in the room didn't seem to want the boyfriend around, so he and the investigators left the area. Lena stayed behind, perfectly comfortable being by herself in the room. She picked up a set of dowsing rods one of the investigators had left for her, and started asking questions.

The rods were reacting very well, crossing strongly when Lena asked questions, and straightening themselves properly when asked. At one point, Lena asked, "Do you like having me down here?" The rods crossed in an emphatic "yes".

Then Lena felt a hand graze her cheek in an unmistakable caress. She grabbed the walkie-talkie and keyed the mic.

"Can someone come and get me?" She kept her voice calm.

"Sure. Why?"

"Because I just felt someone touch my face, and obviously no one's down here."

Katie Metcalf, one of the historians at the Pollak Hospital, had a unique experience in the Men's Ward. It was very late on a public tour night, about half past midnight. Some of the ghost hunters had already tapped out. Katie went on a walkthrough of the building to see who was still there.

The whole building had been lights-out for the past several hours. The Men's Death Ward was dark, lit only by one small night light on the wall. The room is always furnished with benches, and they are not only for audiences to sit on to watch the slide shows. The benches also serve another purpose: investigators are encouraged to lie down on the benches and imagine what it would have been like to lie in a stark hospital bed in that very room, your only view the white acoustic ceiling tiles overhead, and to know that you had only weeks or days to live.

The Men's Death Ward could hold two hundred and fifty patients. That sounds like a lot to cram into the space, but the cots were six feet long, and only about two feet wide. When you're dying of tuberculosis, you don't move around much.

Katie walked quietly into the dark room. She didn't want to interrupt if the investigators were doing an EVP session. She listened for voices in the quiet …

… but all she heard was the soft rasping of someone snoring.

Oh great, Katie thought. *Yeah, it's late, but honestly!*

Not trying to be quiet any longer, Katie went out into the hall and slapped the light switch, hoping that the flood of light would wake the sleeper up.

Katie went back into the ward—to find it was completely empty.

Michelle Battey was walking around in the Men's Ward on an investigation when she suddenly stopped. She simply felt like she couldn't go any farther. There were a couple of Pollak guides in the room with the ghost hunters. Michelle told the guides about her strange experience. They looked at each other knowingly.

"This was by the garage doors, wasn't it?"

"Yes, right there," Michelle confirmed.

The guides nodded. They'd had their own run-ins with that invisible presence.

The ghost hunting group Ghost Duck visited the Pollak on August 18, 2017. During the tour of the building, Christina led the small group into the Men's Ward. The investigator running the camera spoke up.

"Do you feel that?" he asked the rest of the group.

"What?" "As soon as I walked in, my chest started getting all itchy and tingly," the investigator said. "I like that!"

(Yes, paranormal investigators tend to be odd folks. We feel something weird in a walkthrough, we're gonna get excited rather than freaked out.)

Orbs have a rather tarnished reputation in the world of paranormal investigation. There are some people that get super jazzed whenever an orb shows up. There are other people that refuse to acknowledge that an orb is anything other than a dust mote, or a bug really close to the camera.

I'm somewhere in the middle. (Okay, I skew a little closer to "dust mote" dismissal.) I'll give an orb photo a chance, if I must. I'll take a closer look at a video that claims to have an orb in it. How about that? Would you believe an actual moving video of an orb?

How about a video of an orb that lasts longer than most Hollywood movies?

Christina Morris is not only the historian of the Peoria State Hospital; she also does a fair amount of ghost hunting. And quite a lot of that happens in the Pollak Hospital. One night, she was doing an investigation in the hospital with three other volunteers, a couple of the building's owners, and two members of a ghost hunting group. Everyone wanted to do most of their investigating in the basement, so that's where the group spent most of the evening. They did set up a camera in the Men's Ward, just to see what would happen. The camera picked up a bright white orb that floated around a corner of the room—at about the very same place where the Thingie was captured, as a matter of fact. It meandered aimlessly, not following any particular pattern, not darting as an insect would, but floating down and then back up again.

The orb wandered around that corner of the room for *three hours.*

Nick Sarlo, of Shadow Hunters, had a very interesting encounter with a spirit in the Men's Ward. The group had gathered in the ward to do a spirit box session—but they never even got started. Liz Nygard, Nick's colleague, is a very powerful medium. (She's one of those gifted people who can see spirits. She once had a conversation with someone in a laundromat, and chatted with the lady for several hours without realizing the woman was dead.)

Nick had the spirit box out, and he decided to sit on one of the benches in the Men's Ward. "I could see all these different spirits in the middle of the first and second benches," Liz told me. "There was no time to tell him that someone was already sitting there."

Nick sat down—right in the middle of a spirit who didn't have time to get out of the way. Liz explains the sensation graphically. "It's like experiencing an entire roller coaster ride in the space of a few seconds—both for you and the spirit. I still don't know how Nick didn't throw up. Probably because he's totally into roller coasters." We did have to take him back to Command Central and pour a Pixie Stik down his gullet. Here's a ghost hunting tip for you: chocolate may work on Dementors, but when you're just feeling drained or woozy during an investigation, there's nothing like a quick shot of pure flavored sugar to revive you. Bring Pixie Stiks. Seriously.

One of the many groups that have filmed in the halls and wards of the Pollak is Evidence: Paranormal. Their founder, Nathan Galler, recorded a wonderful episode of their YouTube series at the Pollak. He sent me a long, gracious email when I asked his permission to include his show in this book.

"I'd be honored. If it brings a little respect back to the former residents, former employees and their families then I'm extremely grateful.

"I want my films to be informative and bring awareness that just because we don't understand the paranormal doesn't mean we should fear it. I choose to be a little more compassionate about every location because I feel the location, its history and possibly its resident spirits all deserve so much better."

Evidence: Paranormal visited the Pollak Hospital on September 4, 2015 as part of an American Hauntings tour. Nathan was the lead investigator, accompanied by Mary Bland. Right from the jump, the two knew that the building would be a rich source of activity that night. Early in the evening, Mary began to have trouble breathing in the hallway outside the Men's Death Ward. (If you've gotten this far in the book, you know that this is not unusual.)

"There's pressure on my chest," Mary reported with a frown. "It's hard to breathe." She eventually had to leave the building for a while to get her breath back. After sitting outside with the bugs of early September for ten minutes, she was ready to face the hallways again.

The two were able to explore the building for the rest of the evening. "For us, the approach is respect, and never provocation. They deserve that much," Nathan explained.

In the Men's Ward, Nathan gave a lovely monologue to whatever spirits happened to be listening. The gist of his speech was this: all humans have energy. The difference between us and the dead is that we still have vessels. And the nebulous energy forms of the dead, well, that can be whatever they've imagined for themselves. They can appear as they did in their youth, or when they passed, or maybe even both.

Nathan's impromptu speech seemed to strike a chord with someone in the Men's Ward. He had an Ovilus running, which spits out words somewhat in the way a spirit box does. But an Ovilus can be set to "phonetic mode", which presents syllables one at a time. After Nathan had said his piece, the Ovilus burped out "Nate …", and Nathan glanced at the camera.

The Ovilus finished, "…than." Nathan cocked an eyebrow at the camera.

Someone had been paying attention.

THE WOMEN'S WARD

The energy in the Women's Ward has traditionally been gentler, more low-key than in the Men's Ward. Something about the kitchen scene, though, really stirred up a lot of energy. Maybe it was Evan, Brian and I recreating a brutal attack for several months of Saturday nights that did it, I don't know. But someone was pretty agitated for a good long while.

During one walkthrough, a group of ghost hunters were going through the kitchen scene. There are enough volunteers that work at the Pollak that during investigations, there is a guide at every one of the building's hot spots—Men's Ward, Women's Ward, and basement—in case the investigators need any help or have questions about the building or about the asylum's history in general. Another guide was acting as the "caboose", a volunteer that stays at the back of the tour to be the last person out of a room.

Someone in the group said, "Can you give us a sign that you're here?" The kitchen scene included a row of utensils hanging on hooks above the counter, to give the scene a bit of set dressing. When the investigator asked that question, a large serving spoon detached itself from its hook and flew across the room in a clatter of metal. The caboose decided she'd had enough at that point, and left hurriedly down the hallway in search of Christina.

The kitchen scene is long gone, replaced by another gory set from the rich imagination of the haunt designers who transform the building for the Haunted Infirmary every October. But the spirits continue to make their presence known.

James Barrow visited the Pollak in May 2016. The spirits in the Women's Ward were in a chatty mood that night. James was using a spirit box to communicate, so the recordings he captured that night are considered RVPs (radio voice phenomena) rather than EVPs (electronic voice phenomena). The voices were coming through loud and clear. The spirits he had encountered on his many visits to the Bowen seemed to seek him out at the Pollak.

> *"James, it's Michael."*
> *"Sarah, from the Bowen."*
> *"We've been trying to talk to you."*

Isen, a young autistic boy, is a frequent visitor to the Pollak. One afternoon, he was with Christina Morris and a few other guests in the Women's Ward, and he kept trying to get Christina's attention. "Nine, nine," he repeated. Isen doesn't just repeat random numbers without a reason; that's not how his flavor of autism works. Christina kept asking him, "Nine what?" By way of explanation, Isen simply swept his arm out, gesturing to indicate the room where the group was standing.

That night, a ghost hunting group toured the Pollak. One of the investigators asked the spirit box, "How many spirits are here with us tonight?"

The answer came back, "*Nine.*"

Christina was one of the guides that night, and she was stunned by the spirit box's answer. She thought to herself, boy, this kid's really got it. And later, the investigators went back to the hallway outside the Women's Ward.

"Are there nine spirits here tonight?"

"*Yes,*" the spirit box assured her.

"It was just as clear as a bell," Christina told me later. "And I didn't even tell the investigator what Isen had said earlier that day."

Michelle Battey was exploring the Women's Ward when she had a sudden desire to start pacing the floor. "There were pulses of restless energy just surging through me," she told me. Her theory, and it's a good one, is that she was picking up on the relentless wandering urges of some of the female geriatric patients who called the Pollak home in the last days of the Peoria State Hospital.

Speaking of geriatric patients, it seems the Dirty Girl is still around. I wrote about the Dirty Girl in *Fractured Spirits*, but here's a refresher.

Shortly after acquiring the Pollak Hospital, the owners were curious about this allegedly haunted building they'd just bought. They asked Christina Morris to lead them on a ghost hunt, so they could experience for themselves what investigators were searching for on their visits. One of these gentlemen, Joe, was the winner of the local Tough Man Contest four years running. This guy was built like a football player. "Arms that would take you down in a second, and a punch that would knock you straight out," as Christina puts it.

As the owners and their wives were wandering around in the Women's Ward, Christina was telling them a bit about the history of the asylum and about the Pollak. During a lull in the talk, Joe came up to Christina with a question.

"These ghosts … can they touch your … stuff?"

"They're ghosts, Joe. They can touch whatever they want," Christina replied.

"No, really, I'm serious—can they touch your … you know, your junk? Your, um, family jewels?"

Christina shrugged. "Again—they're ghosts. If they wanna touch you, they're gonna touch you."

"Because someone's got a handful of my equipment right now," Joe admitted, his big body slightly hunched with the unfamiliar groping sensation.

"Let me see," his wife said, and grabbed a nearby EMF meter. She held it near her husband's crotch, and the meter pegged into the red. She swung it away and held it at arm's length, and the needle fell back into the green. Again, she brought the meter below the belt, and the meter shrieked into the red again. She backed off, and the meter dropped back to green.

At that point, Joe decided he was done ghost hunting for the evening. "I'm out. They can touch all y'all. I'll be outside."

(In case there are any guys reading this who are considering a trip to the Pollak for some spectral action of a physical nature, maybe planning to reenact Dan Aykroyd's one scene from the original *Ghostbusters*, I do feel obliged to tell you this: we have documentation that one of the geriatric patients housed at the Pollak was a 90 year old woman who would regularly strip off all her clothes and go streaking through the hallway. So our Dirty Girl may very well be a Dirty Old Lady. Just some food for thought.)

In July 2016, the Pollak was the site of a two-day investigation, a collaboration between three paranormal groups: Shadow Hunters, from the northern Chicago suburbs, Archer Paranormal Investigations, out of Georgia, and ESP (Explorers of Spirit Phenomena), from Florida. Having been duly warned on the walkthrough about the Dirty Girl, of course the first place the guys wanted to go was the Women's Ward. We all traipsed down there and set Nick and Pat at one end of the room, while we ladies all stood well back from the boys, to give the Dirty Girl some encouragement.

Soon, the detector in front of the guys started to chirp, and both Nick and Pat reported that they were being groped. (They were standing close together, so maybe the ghost had one hand on each of their … you know what? I'm just going to leave it there. Best not to speculate too closely.) Terri Rohde crouched next to Nick and held an EMF meter near his pants, and the needle jumped up about halfway, letting us all know that *something* was going on down there.

We all had a good laugh at the boys being in such a compromising position. Even Pat and Nick saw the humor in the situation. We were all laughing and cracking jokes for the camera, when Nick jumped, and it had nothing to do with the Dirty Girl's attentions.

"Hey, hey, hey, hey!" he yelped. A huge wooden spool, the kind that's used to wind up telephone wire, rolled towards him about six inches, then rocked back about four inches the other way. No one was within three feet of the spool when it moved.

HALLWAYS AND EXAM ROOMS

When the Pollak Hospital was built in 1949, it was designed expressly for the purpose of treating tuberculosis. The other hospitals on the hilltop had treated patients for the disease from the very beginning, and tent colonies for tuberculosis treatment had been set up on the land where the Pollak now sits. The batwing hospital also occupied that spot of land. But the Pollak was purpose-built to care for consumptive patients. It was built in an H-shape, with the Men's and Women's Wards forming the legs of the H, and the long hallway connecting the wards. Small exam rooms lined both sides of the hallway, for oxygen therapy, blood draws, physical exams, and all the other daily routines of the hospital. The wards—the legs of the H—were arranged so that one ward caught the light of the rising sun in the morning, and the other got the light of the setting sun in the evening.

Spirits roam freely in the hallway of the Pollak, and make their presence known in many of the rooms off the hallway. You can walk down the hallway and listen in at closed doors, and hear voices behind those doors.

The two wings of the building are mirror images of each

other. There were tub rooms on each end of the building, where patients received hydrotherapy. In the tub room closest to the Women's Ward, an investigator with Dale Kaczmarek's group recorded a heartbreaking EVP of a woman sobbing in the room. Similar EVPs have been recorded in the delousing exit on the Women's Ward side of the building.

Tuberculosis germs are carried on the clothes, and in the hair. When female patients were admitted, if they had long hair, it was cut short. This may be the reason a female spirit is weeping.

"A woman's hair was her crowning glory," Christina Morris points out. "Whether or not she recovered from being sick, this patients' hair had been cut off. She had given up her hair willingly, hoping that it would help rid her of this terrible sickness—but the loss still caused great sorrow."

Dale Kaczmarek and members of Ghost Research Society were in the Tub Room on the Women's Ward side, when they heard noises out in the hallway. Dale, being the savvy investigator that he is, didn't want to alert the spirits to his presence and give them the chance to hide.

"I didn't lean out into the hallway. I just stuck my hand out, holding the camera, and snapped a few pictures. I got mist on three of them, then the next two, nothing, nothing."

Before the current owners bought the building, the Pollak was home to a couple of businesses. When NEPCO had their offices in the building, the employees had a pet cat named "Blackie". Blackie was a great mouser, and he had the run of the building. He was very affectionate, and took every opportunity to rub up against people's legs when he encountered them in the hallway.

As a matter of fact, Blackie still does that today, decades after his death.

Even when NEPCO employees still worked in the building, they spoke fondly of hearing Blackie's friendly meow in the hallway, even after he'd used up his ninth life. They'd see him, too, a black shadow against the darkness. Blackie has shown himself to investigators too. They have experienced the same phenomena as the NEPCO employees did: hearing the soft meow of a phantom puss, feeling a friendly brush against a leg, and seeing a cat-sized shadow dart down the hallway.

Maybe Blackie is still chasing ghost mice on the Other Side.

James Barrow's visit in May 2016 yielded a wealth of EVPs and RVPs in various exam rooms. In one room, he caught several snippets of spirit conversation.

"Josh! I'm Josh. I'm from Coney Island."

"Her name's Laura."

"Go find it." (This one sounds like a nurse or a young doctor impatiently giving an order: "Go *find* it."

"We're dead."

"Help me find Daddy."

A different room had another young spirit hiding in it. James stepped into the room and went fishing.

"My name's Jim, can you tell me your name?"

Immediately a child's voice crooned, *"Hello."*

"What's your name, little girl?" James encouraged.

He heard a very faint *"Rhoda"*, then a soft giggle.

In another exam room, James asked if patients were treated there. The KII meter he was holding flashed. Investigators usually interpret that as the spirits trying to give an affirmative answer, so James noted for his recorder that the KII had gone off. Then, naturally, he added, "I'd call that a yes." He quickly got an EVP in response that snapped, *"That's not a yes!"*

James then asked a couple of questions about the haunted house. "Do you think it's fun?"

"Kind of."

"Is it scary?"

"Kind of," the spirit said diffidently. (Listening to these, I can imagine a shrug of invisible shoulders.)

Soon after this, the guide in charge of that area had a coughing fit. James seized the moment and tried to see if any of the spirits hanging around were medical staff rather than patients. "We need a nurse out here, got a guy choking," James called out to the air.

A spirit responded with brisk efficiency.

"Who's choking?"

"The first time I got bum-rushed by a bunch of ghosts I was at the Pollak outside of the Men's Ward."

The triple threat of Shadow Hunters, ESP, and Archer Paranormal Investigations had several memorable experiences in the hallway and exam rooms. Liz Nygard, then of Shadow Hunters, actually heard the horde of spirits rushing towards her.

"I was in the hallway with Alexi [another Shadow Hunters member] and it sounded like a stampede. It was extraordinary. Alexi actually felt a cool breeze. You remember how hot that place was in July. Alexi was excited because she felt cold, and it felt good.

"It was like something out of a movie for me. Hundreds of souls racing down the hallway. I turned to Alexi and said, 'This is the part where we go,' and we quickly ducked into the Men's Ward. It was just rather intense."

Liz was with Lisa Shackelford when they had another encounter in the hallway—although neither of them were aware of it at the time.

Lisa told me the story, which actually started well outside the building. "We were all eating lunch at the Pizza Ranch in Peoria before we came back to the Pollak for the second day of investigation. I heard someone say 'dearly beloved' right in my ear. My guides have a good sense of humor, because I heard it again. Terri and Tracy were looking at me oddly, and I said, 'I just think we should go and play music in the building when we get there.'"

Music can be one of the most powerful tools in a ghost hunter's box of tricks. How many times have you been transported to another place, another time, just by hearing the first few notes of a beloved song (or even a song you just can't stand)? Music can have a powerful effect on us—even after we've passed on. If spirits can hear us talking, they can darn sure hear us playing music too.

"We got to the building, and because of the 'dearly beloved' thing, I called up Prince's song 'Let's Go Crazy'. Everyone loves Prince, even people who've been dead for a hundred years," Lisa said with a grin.

It must be true, because the music got someone's attention,

and it was caught on film. In the clip, Lisa and Liz are standing in the hallway with another investigator, next to the piano, smiling as the catchy music fills the air. A shadow figure walks out of the wall to Lisa's left. It comes toward the group, then disappears. 👻

Music also played a huge role in a stunning encounter that night in the Doll Room. The Doll Room is one of the more active rooms in the building anyway. The room is crammed with dozens of dolls, a few of which are actually haunted. (When asked, Christina Morris will politely but very firmly refuse to tell you which dolls are the haunted ones. She just requests that you don't touch *any* of them, just to be safe.)

The Doll Room is an exam room, like many of the rooms off the hallway. It isn't very big. A dozen investigators might be able to fit, if they all exhale. We wedged as many of us as we could into the small room. I was standing near the door that leads to the adjacent exam room. Other investigators sat on the floor, and a lucky few found chairs. We were all too big to fit in the child-size rocking chair, so we left it alone.

Someone fired up an iPod, and the cameras started rolling. We played Adele's "Hello" because honestly, how could you not? With lyrics like "Hello from the other side", I mean really, it's almost guaranteed to get some kind of reaction. More Prince rounded out the playlist. The musician had passed over just a couple of months before this, in April 2016, so we all thought it was fitting to invite the spirits to "party like it's 1999". If we were hoping to increase spirit activity by playing fun, upbeat music, we sure got our wish that night.

One investigator, Becca, felt the presence of a young girl cuddling close to her. She is the mother of a toddler, so maybe this little spirit child recognized her as a maternal figure. Becca was so overcome by the child's trusting embrace that she had to excuse herself and retreat to Command Central (the safe room) to get her composure back.

But Becca's encounter with the young ghost affected her so powerfully and personally that she simply had to leave the building. She drove home soon after that, and hasn't been back since then.

By that time, "1999" was over, and the next song started to

play. I was jazzed to hear that it was one of my favorite Prince songs, "Raspberry Beret".

It was while this song was playing that we noticed that the small rocking chair was moving on its own. This was a real bucket list moment for me—that's one of my favorite horror movie tropes, and I've been aching to see a rocking chair rocking by itself for decades. I guess the peppy Prince music did the trick! 👻

(Shadow Hunters turned their investigation of the Pollak Hospital into the first episode of their YouTube show. Please visit their channel to see the shadow figure in the hallway, the rocking chair, and of course, Nick and Pat getting felt up by the Dirty Girl.)

One winter evening, Christina Morris and a few Pollak volunteers were hanging out in the bathroom, just off the foyer of the main entrance to the building. (If this seems a bit … well, *odd*, as a choice of gathering places, keep in mind that this story takes place in the winter, in an unheated building. The john is the only warm room in the joint.) The day's work was over, so they were all sitting around in the bathroom talking, like ya do. As they talked, they all heard a knock on the front door.

Brian went out into the foyer, and came back moments later, saying he hadn't seen anyone at the door. The upper half of the front door is clear glass, and the door is flanked on both sides with two more big, clear windows. There's a light above the door, so it's really easy to tell at a glance if there's someone outside.

The conversation picked back up, and again, everyone heard a series of knocks on the front door. Some other luckless volunteer was tapped to go into the cold foyer to investigate. Again, there was no one there. Christina was convinced that a prankster was playing a game of ding-dong ditch, until someone pointed to the concrete steps of the front porch. While everyone was inside chatting, it had started to snow, and now there was an inch or two of pristine snow on the steps and ramp outside the door.

Not one footprint marred the freshly fallen snow.

Christina was with another group of volunteers when they had a similar experience at the back door. Everyone was huddled in one of the green oxygen scrubber rooms in the Men's Ward, the one on the right side as you're facing the back door of the ward. A bunch of people were headed down the sidewalk path to Cemetery Two, which is very close to that end of the building, and Christina was trying to decipher what they were saying.

Someone rattled the doorknob of the outside door, and everyone sighed impatiently. They thought it was Jeff, Christina's husband, trying to scare them. The doorknob rattled again.

"Jeff, cut it out!" Christina whisper-yelled through the door. "Be quiet—we're trying to make sure the people in the cemetery are gone!"

They slowly opened the door, exposing a dark empty closet, just as Jeff came into the ward—from outside. He'd been nowhere near the door.

Close to the mysteriously opening locked door across from the Men's Ward is the Delousing Exit. This plays an important part in the history of the Pollak Hospital ... and in its ghost lore.

When patients were admitted to the Pollak, they came in through this door, which is at the back of the building. It opens onto a small entrance hall, which opens into the hallway very near the Men's Ward. There's an identical entrance on the women's side. The patients were met by a nurse. They were asked to disrobe, and their clothes were taken directly back out that door and burned. If a female patient had long hair, it was cut short. Tuberculosis germs, as noted before, are carried on the clothing and hair, so the hospital staff was trying to reduce the spread of the disease with these drastic measures. Then a nurse took the patient across the hall to a small room, where they were given hydrotherapy consisting of a hot bath, followed by a cold shower. This opened up the bronchial tubes in the lungs, allowing the patient to breathe more easily. Then the patient would be given a hospital robe and escorted across the hall to another room for a preliminary exam.

When the Pollak tour included re-creations of historic scenes, this was one of the most powerful bits of acting. Christina would stand at the door and describe the intake process. As she did so, an actress portraying a young girl came in through the door. She wore her hair in long braids, and she clutched a doll for comfort. She was met at the entrance by a nurse who escorted her across the hall and closed the door. All this time, Christina was talking about what patients experienced when they arrived. As Christina continued her talk, the door opened, and the nurse gently guided the young girl back across the hall to an exam room adjacent to the entrance. The girl still cuddled her doll, but now she wore a hospital gown instead of a dress—and her long hair was gone, chopped close to her head. She walked with the nurse, shorn head bowed, into the exam room. It was a very touching scene, dramatic in its simplicity.

One evening, I happened to be there with a group, and we stood around in the hallway as Christina did her history thing. Dee played the part of the young girl, and Jackie portrayed the caring nurse. Dee came out of the room, hair chopped short, and Jackie took her shoulders to lead her to the exam room, where Dee sat on the exam table. Both women, their action parts over, relaxed a bit. They were still "on scene", but the scene didn't require anything else from them, so they just sat quietly in the room as Christina continued to talk.

Suddenly, Christina's monologue was interrupted by two deep, rasping, ragged, tubercular breaths. All of us in the hallway looked at each other, a bit uncomfortable. I'd seen that scene a dozen times or so by that point, and Dee had never added sound effects to her performance. We all thought, "Boy, Dee is really pouring it on tonight!" Meanwhile, in the exam room, Dee and Jackie stared at each other, completely nonplussed. "Are they making *fun* of me out there?" Dee muttered. "Rude!"

If you guessed that none of us made those deep dramatic breaths, give yourself a gold star.

Michelle Battey may have had an encounter with the same little girl experienced by Weapons, Becca, and James Barrow. Michelle was standing in the room just to the right of the foyer—the room from which Weapons heard the mumbled voice of a young girl—when she became aware of a little girl's presence. *"Don't go down into the basement,"* the girl warned. Now, whether she was actually frightened of one of the spirits down there, or if she'd been told in life to keep out of the basement, Michelle couldn't say.

THE BASEMENT

But Michelle *did* go down into the basement. And it would be a shame not to. Some of the richest experiences in the Pollak happen in the basement. The door to the electrical room still slams shut with regularity, as reported in *Fractured Spirits*. The black metal door is now decorated with white sigils that look vaguely exotic and a bit disconcerting—until Christina explains to you that they were drawn in caulk on the door as a prop for one of the horror shorts they've filmed down there. (In case you're wondering, the symbols are all variations of "good fortune".)

There was also a salt circle on the concrete floor for a short while. That was another prop. It's long gone, of course, but it formed the basis of an absolutely endearing story. Christina Morris got a call from a guy who wanted to book a tour for himself and his girlfriend. The girlfriend loved the paranormal, she just couldn't get enough of ghost hunting shows on tv, so the guy figured it would make a great anniversary present for her. Pollak volunteers drew the circle—an exercise familiar to any fan of *Supernatural*—and when the tour got down to the basement, the two of them got into the protective circle. Christina told a ghostly story, then the room was plunged into semi-darkness as they cut the lights. The only light came from the flickering candles held by the "tour nurses", all in costume. The girl suddenly realized that her boyfriend, still holding her hand, had dropped to one knee.

"You'll never have to be afraid," he promised her. "I will always be by your side. Will you marry me?"

There wasn't a dry eye in the room.

The rough spirit is down there still as well. This is the spirit mentioned in *Fractured Spirits* as a bully, who likes to hurt people. We've learned more about this spirit over the years. Psychic mediums and paranormal investigators know that if a person was a jerk in life, they're likely going to be an unpleasant spirit after they've passed on. Personalities don't seem to change very much after death. We've gotten the impression that this spirit's gruffness may be just a personality trait that he retained after death. It doesn't mean that he's evil, just that he's ... prickly.

Michelle Battey wandered into the electrical room on her visit to the Pollak basement. She heard the clicking of long-gone electrical relays, and the busy hum of machinery. She looked around, curious. She didn't see anyone, but she got the distinct feeling that someone was in there with her—and he didn't like it.

"It was like he was saying, 'Go away. Can't you see I'm busy?' I got the feeling he was just too busy to be bothered with us. Like he had work to do, and we investigators were getting in his way."

There may be a very interesting historical connection to this crusty, antisocial spirit, and a rather salacious one at that. During an EVP session several years ago, Christina and some other investigators caught an EVP that demanded to know, *"Where are the whores?"* That caused even Christina to raise an eyebrow. There was much discussion among the (mostly female) ghost hunters. Did the spirit mean ... them? That was a disquieting thought.

In her continuous research on the asylum's history, Christina found an answer to the suggestive question. She discovered that up until the 1950s, when ladies of the evening were picked up in Peoria for streetwalking, they were often required to do community service at the Peoria State Hospital as part of their sentence. (One wonders exactly what these ladies' definition of "community service" was.)

Interestingly, this practice started well before the Peoria State Hospital even existed. It actually dates back to the early 1800s, and started in England. Prostitution was one of those crimes where women were required to work their community service hours in a workhouse, almshouse, or mental institution, places where people required care. No one wanted to care for the elderly or the mentally ill so, if a prostitute wound up in court and the judge realized she had a decent intellect, rather than send her to prison (which was often a death sentence, given the wretched conditions of prisons at the time), the judge would send her to a mental hospital to work off her sentence as an attendant. Judges saw this as a way for women to repay their debt to society. It was basically a source of free labor. It's easy to see, though, how patients at most institutions suffered from substandard care, when the people caring for them were either poorly-paid employees or criminal "volunteers".

Dr. Zeller, with his deep respect for women, encouraged the practice at the Peoria State Hospital. He believed passionately in the worth of all women, so he acquiesced when judges sent ladies of the evening to the hilltop to work off their sentences. The asylum accepted this free source of patient care until the early 1950s.

Paranormal investigator Marcia Mack, who posts on YouTube as Ghosthunter Marcia, led a group down to the basement, and they captured several EVPs on their visit. Not only did they get EVPs, but they also experienced audible phenomena too, whispers, mutters, even the odd moan. Marcia got touched in the basement, and they picked up several EVPs that could very well have come from the grumpy guy in the electrical room.

Over the course of their visit to the basement, Marcia and her group heard, *"You're in trouble"*, *"Get away"*, *"I want you to leave"*, *"I … give up"*, and *"Trying … to shut 'em up"* (this one actually came from the direction of the electrical room). It sounded like the rough spirit was in an especially irritable mood that evening.

Ghosthunter Marcia has another Pollak video on YouTube, filmed after the Paranormal Kicks Cancer event held at the Pollak in 2012. This event brought together groups from all over Illinois, so Marcia was joined by Into the Night Paranormal, IPRA, Chicago Paranormal, West Chicago Paranormal, and renowned investigator Chris Fleming, among others. Marcia's group was again down in the basement, and the spirits were again in fine form.

As they walked into the cold storage room, a spirit

commented *"We're walking … behind her."* An interesting thing to hear when you're exploring a haunted basement!

Later, Marcia commented to the spirits, "Todd [another member of the group] does not believe that you exist." Todd spoke up to defend himself. "I believe, I just need proof." Two spirits responded to this clarification. One muttered, *"Bullshit."* Another voice gave the opinion, *"They're both nuts."*

Chris Fleming was part of Marcia's group, and he was getting some wonderful action from an SB7 spirit box. At one point, he asked if there was a spirit present. The ghost box spat out *"Yeah", "Yes", "I'm here"* in quick succession—almost as if the entity wanted to make sure they didn't get overlooked.

Fleming was also the target of some concern from the spirit world a bit later. The evening was wearing on, and Marcia caught Fleming yawning widely, not even trying to hide it. (Hey, investigations can go on for *hours.*) Marcia joked, "I'm going to make a montage of just Chris yawning."

"Sorry," Chris mumbled with a sheepish grin. The spirit box in his hand piped up with a suggestion.

"Need sleep."

The gruff spirit may be one of several male entities in the basement. When Michelle Battey, Diane Lockhart, and I were downstairs one night, a male spirit approached Diane. Something about his demeanor made Diane nervous, so she snapped, "Don't touch me!" Michelle later became aware of this spirit pouting in the corner after Diane's rebuke.

The spirit of the young girl seems to be around yet, too. A Pollak volunteer named Ashley told me about an experience she had with Sam Callear. The two of them were down in the basement during the day. They were in the first room of the basement, which has a couple of ground-floor windows. These windows, dirty as they are with the grime of decades, let a bit of daylight into that first room. Sam happened to be standing near a window, with his hand in a beam of light. In that sliver of light, Ashley saw a small hand reach out and grab Sam's hand.

"He felt the hand touch him, and it spooked him," Ashley told me. An unexpected touch *would* be spooky. Sam seems to attract that sort of attention in the basement. For another of Sam's experiences, please see *Fractured Spirits.*

One of the interesting games Pollak volunteers have developed to interact with the spirits in the basement is a version of Ring Around the Rosie. The ghost hunters form a circle for the game, but they leave a space in the ring. They start singing and walking in a circle, keeping that space open as they go … just in case someone wants to jump in and join them.

One evening, the space in the ring was between Jill and Jackie, right across from Ashley. The young volunteer told me what happened next.

"I saw a dark figure in the shape of a grown man. He was taller than Jackie, and he was standing right *there* in the space between them."

SIC (Supernatural Investigation Crew) visited the Pollak in January 2018. While in the basement, the team set up an SLS camera, one that shows the spirits as red stick figures. We were astounded to see a couple of figures show up on the screen. One of them was sitting crouched on the floor, which intrigued us all because Diane had said earlier that Rhoda Derry was a frequent visitor to the basement. The figure crawled over to a chair and hoisted itself onto the seat. It repeated this action about three times.

Bill Topalovic, then a member of SIC, wandered into the electrical room. The SLS camera was still catching stick figures; the investigators had pointed it towards the corner of the room, and the door to the electrical room was in the frame as well. Diane assured us that the grouchy electrician was still in "his" room. Bill paid no attention to this. It was his first investigation, so he was just taking it all in.

Bill was standing in the doorway of the electrical room considering where to go next, when he felt a slight pressure on his left shoulder. Then he heard everyone else in the basement gasp. He looked up to find everyone staring at him.

"He's touching you."

"What?"

"He's touching you!"

"Where?"

"On the shoulder." Bill was, frankly, a bit worried by then.

"Which shoulder?"

"The left one."

Did I mention this was Bill's first investigation? He told me later that he didn't want to be "that guy", so he said he couldn't be sure if he'd felt anything or not.

He didn't stick around in the room, though.

Bill did have an experience with the SLS camera that made his first investigation memorable. The investigators saw the red stick figure on the camera screen and tried to interact with it.

"We asked it to raise its arms or stand; it did not. We asked it to set the motion detector on the floor off; it did not. We asked again—a red leg shot out and the sensor went off. *This* was my 'aha' moment," Bill told me.

I've mentioned the investigation that took place over two sweltering days in July 2016, with ESP, Archer Paranormal Investigations, and Shadow Hunters all experiencing the Pollak. On the second day, a couple of the female investigators decided to dress up as doctors, essentially turning themselves into walking, talking trigger objects. The costumes were simple but unmistakable; both women wore white lab coats and had stethoscopes slung around their necks.

Several of us went down to the basement, and decided to start off our session with some EVP work in the electrical room. Someone set up a camera—facing out of the electrical room into the cold storage room—and we sat in the chairs that are always set up in the small room for investigators to use. I forget exactly who was there; there were five or six of us, including Lisa Shackelford and myself. Lisa was one of the two women dressed as doctors.

Camera running, we started our EVP session. We'd been sitting there asking questions for a few minutes when Lisa, who was sitting in the second chair from the end, let out a yelp like she'd just stepped on a Lego. It scared the paste out of me, and I jumped like a scalded cat, because I was in the chair on the end of the row, right next to Lisa. All of us turned to Lisa with frantic shrieks—"What? What happened?"

Something had slipped the stethoscope from around Lisa's neck. "This was a professional stethoscope. It had some weight to it. It literally pulled right off of me. Made me squeal!"

Lisa is no stranger to the spirit world. She's a powerful psychic medium, who is very comfortable with her gifts. "I'm used to spirits fiddling with my hair, giving me the occasional poke." This was the first time, though, that a spirit had interacted with her so dramatically.

"I'm glad they were so open to me there."

There was one thing, though, that irritated every single one of us. The camera, of course, had been pointing the opposite way, out of the room, facing the cold storage room. We didn't capture the mysteriously moving stethoscope.

Ain't that always the way?

The basement of the Pollak is unquestionably a very active place. Sensitives feel the presence of several entities down there, each with their own unique personality.

And sometimes, those spirits are so eager to communicate that they reach out to us ... and introduce themselves.

THE BOY IN THE BASEMENT

It all started when a friendly ghost wanted to hold my hand.

I was at the Pollak, doing an investigation with Peoria Paranormal. It was at the end of April, so the air in the building still held a bit of a chill. I had ridden my motorcycle to the building that evening, so I was happy to leave my jacket on as we explored.

Several of us were downstairs in the first basement room, the large room before the cold storage area. We were standing around in a loose circle, with a spirit box on the floor in the center of the group. We were getting a steady stream of good answers from the spirit box, and we were all jazzed with the way the session was going.

For me, it was about to get even better.

I was standing there listening to the burping static of the spirit box. I was holding my recorder flat on my right palm, and I wasn't really doing anything with my left hand; it was just down at my side. During the session, though, I became aware of a warmth stealing over the fingers of my left hand. The feeling was soft at first, almost hesitant. It never reached past my fingers. But soon, I was feeling such insistent heat on my fingers that it felt like I was holding my left hand out to the gently glowing coals of a campfire.

It was a very cozy feeling, but one that I'd never experienced before. We had a sensitive with us that evening. She was standing across the circle from me, so I called her over to my side of the group.

"Something weird is going on over here. It's nothing bad, not at all, just … I need you to tell me what's going on."

She worked her way around the circle and stood close to me. "Yeah, there's someone holding your hand," she confirmed. "Sylvia, you've got a fan!"

Just then a "*yes!*" blurted out of the spirit box.

This was way past cool. It was my first time being touched by a ghost—at least the first time I knew about it. And this spirit seemed friendly; I wasn't scared at all, just really intrigued. We asked the ghost its name, and got the response "*Christopher*" from the spirit box.

"All this guy wants is to be in your book," someone behind me muttered.

The sensitive concentrated for a moment, then smiled. "Actually, yes. That's exactly what he wants."

Several months later, in July of that year, I returned to the basement of the Pollak. I had another psychic with me, a photographer from Los Angeles who had been drawn to the picturesque grandeur of the Bowen Building. I invited her to check out the Pollak as well, and Christina Morris gave us a tour.

In the basement, I held my hand out for Christopher to hold. This time I felt a faint warmth, and a tingling in the palm of my hand. Merilee confirmed for me that this was indeed Christopher. Then she gave me a few more details.

"He's tall, young—I'd say early twenties. He's got dark hair, and he's good-looking." Then she said something I was absolutely *not* expecting to hear.

"He loves you. Not in a romantic way," she hurried to clarify. "You remind him of someone he knew in life. That's why he's attracted to you."

For the next few years, I said hello to Christopher whenever I was down in the basement. I always held my hand out for him to hold, since he seemed to enjoy it so much. Sometimes I felt that tingly warmth, sometimes I didn't. But I couldn't stop thinking about the young man whose life had ended far too soon. I wished for a better way to communicate with this amiable spirit.

Then, one memorable evening, I got my wish. In July 2017, American Hauntings put together one of their tours at the Pollak.

I showed up, because it's always so much fun to explore the building with people who've never been there before. I scanned the group ... and found a familiar face. Diane Lockhart, who shared her experiences with me for *Fractured Spirits*, was on the tour that night. When we split up into groups for our investigation, I nipped over to Diane's side. "I'm with her," I said firmly.

I knew if anyone at the Pollak that night could help me communicate with Christopher, it would be Diane. She is a psychic medium, and one of the most honest, straightforward people I know. Finally, after years of longing, I'd get to talk with the boy in the basement.

We made our way downstairs with a few other investigators—all women, as it turned out. I sat in one chair, Diane in another, and I gestured to the empty chair on my left.

"Christopher, would you like to sit next to me and chat?"

I explained to him that Diane could see and hear him, even though I could not. "We can finally have a conversation, Christopher. I'll ask you questions, and Diane will ... um, she'll tell me what you said."

It still felt very strange to be asking questions of someone I couldn't see. I had to take Diane's word that Christopher had accepted my invitation and was sitting in the chair next to me. And then I had to keep reminding myself to address my questions to the spirit sitting in that chair. It would, admittedly, have been rude to invite him to sit down for a conversation, then ignore the fact that he was sitting there.

We found out, through our conversation, that his name was indeed Christopher, but that he preferred to go by Chris. He admitted to being tall and having dark hair, but he said, "Nobody's ever called me handsome before." He also mentioned that the last year he remembered was 1905.

Now, this is significant. Remember in the last chapter, when I mentioned the sixteen female and ten male patients who spent the winter of 1906 in the tent colony? Was Chris one of those men? Or maybe, was he one of the six patients who survived the winter of 1905 on a cottage porch—or didn't? It's obvious he spent at least one winter in a tent. He clearly described lying in a bed in a tent—he said that if you were in a bed close to the wood-burning stove, it was alright, but if you were farther away, it was really chilly. And Christina Morris, the historian of the asylum, has confirmed that the canvas tents where the tuberculosis patients were housed were indeed heated with stoves. And the wooden floors would have helped to keep the chill down.

Chris wouldn't have been aware of Dr. Zeller's administrative decisions to house tuberculosis patients in tent colonies. He would have just lived—and died—where he was put. We asked him if he knew Dr. Zeller, and he said, "He was a nice man." I had to sit for a while and digest that. *I was having a casual chat with someone who freaking knew Dr. Zeller—one of my personal heroes.*

Then Chris said something that absolutely broke my heart. He mentioned the dances that were held on Saturday nights for the patients, but then he added, "We could hear the music coming from the other cottages, but we couldn't go over and dance." It made sense; the tuberculosis patients were in quarantine for a very good reason. It still made me sad, though, to think of this once-vibrant young man wasting away with tuberculosis, unable even to enjoy the simple pleasure of a dance with a pretty girl.

As I was musing over the unfairness of it all, a few of the other ghost hunters came into the cold storage room. They'd been sitting in the electrical room, and just wanted a change of scenery. One woman went to sit down in the chair next to me, and I stopped her with an outstretched hand. I knew how idiotic it would sound even as I opened my mouth, but the words tumbled out before I could stop them.

"Sorry, but someone's already sitting there."

The woman gave me a look like I was speaking Swahili. Then Diane burst out laughing. "Chris said, 'You didn't *have* to tell her that!'", she giggled.

I gave the chair next to me an arch look. "Cheeky!" I teased him with a smile.

Can you blame the guy, though? I mean, he's been hanging out at the asylum for well over a century. Then here comes this room full of women—and he can finally communicate with them. At that point, I'd be inviting someone to sit on my lap too.

And Chris is a healthy young man … well, except for being dead. We caught a very interesting EVP during that first visit with Chris. Diane said, "He's young, about 22," and directly after that, a spirit voice whispered, *"He was 22."* Now, at first I thought this was Chris saying, *"Guess what? Twenty-two,"*, in response to Diane's statement. But other people who have listened to the EVP have pointed out that the voice is not the same as the others (we've gotten several wonderful EVPs from Chris). They say, and after careful consideration I agree with them, that the voice is saying *"He was 22"*—and that the voice is female. Chris has mentioned that Rhoda Derry visits the basement sometimes. Was this stray voice Rhoda chiming in to affirm Diane's reading?

During that first proper conversation, we also discovered why Chris is so attracted to me. Apparently, I remind him of his sister. He grew up on a farm in Indiana, and was sent to the Peoria State Hospital for some reason—we don't know why, as he didn't tell us.

By the next time Diane and I were at the Pollak, several months later in January 2018, I had figured out a gift for Chris, one that might go a long way toward repaying him for the effort it took for him to speak to us. We came downstairs—the group we were with that night was Aaron Shriver's group Supernatural Investigation Crew (SIC)—and Chris was delighted to see us again. He was still a bit fuzzy on the concept of why Diane could see and hear him perfectly well, and I could not. I tried to explain to him that some people have different talents and abilities: some people can play the violin, some people can bake really good bread, some people can build furniture, and some people can see and hear dead folks. Not everyone can do that, I explained to him. He seemed to accept that, but we had to explain it anew on the next visit.

"I have a surprise for you, Chris," I said once we'd settled down. I'd been ruminating on the pain and boredom and isolation he'd felt as a young man, hearing the cheerful music coming from nearby cottages as the other patients enjoyed their Saturday night dance. I wanted so much to bring him the happy sounds of celebration.

I pulled out my phone—I didn't even try to explain *that* to him—and pulled up a recording I'd made earlier that week. The cheerful sound of a ragtime tune jumped into the air. Diane told me with a puzzled smile, "He's doing something with his hands on his knees ..."

"He's doing the Charleston!" I gasped. I was thrilled that the music I'd chosen for him had brought him such delight. When the song was over, Diane turned to me.

"He says, no one's ever done that for me."

There were several other investigators down there with us, a man and a woman I didn't know, and James Barrow. (James was recording, and caught a couple of lovely EVPs from Chris. At one point, I held my hand out to the air and invited Chris to take my hand. "I wish you *would* take my hand, Chris, because it's January, and it's really cold down here, and when you hold my hand, it's warm and tingly—that's how I know it's you." I didn't feel any warmth that time, so I shoved my hand back into my hoodie pocket. James told me later that he caught an EVP of Chris saying, "*Sorry Sylvia, I have no heat.*") The other investigators conferred in low voices, then the guy spoke up.

"Do you think Chris would like to hear a more modern song?"

"I don't see why not," I replied. "He seems to like music in general, and he'd probably enjoy the variety."

The guy held up his phone, and a peppy pop tune started. Being a child of the 80s, I instantly recognized the brassy saxophone intro to "Waiting For A Star To Fall", by Boy Meets Girl. I let out a happy squeal.

"Ooh, this is a good one, Chris, you're gonna like it."

(Later, we discovered that James caught another EVP at that point—Chris saying, "*I do like it.*" He also caught the little girl pleading, "*I want to sing.*")

Later, more members of Supernatural Investigation Crew came down to the basement. James Barrow came down too. James asked Chris (through Diane), "Do you remember me?", and Diane said, "Yes, he definitely remembers you."

Bill Topalovic, a member of SIC, spoke up with a sly grin. "Do you remember *me*, Chris?" I saw him glance at Diane, and I knew his question wasn't so much a question for Chris as it was a test for Diane.

Diane's voice held a little hesitation as she answered for Chris. "He says, *you've* never been here before." Her voice managed to convey Chris's "Aw, mister, you're puttin' me on" tone.

The truthful answer seemed to satisfy Bill, and he puttered around setting up the group's equipment. He'd tested Diane earlier in the evening, when we were all up in the front hallway taking a break. He made no secret about his skepticism. Bill's a very no-nonsense guy, and I could sense his curiosity about exactly how far Diane's talents could stretch. Over the course of the evening, her quiet confidence spoke volumes. By the end of the evening, the skeptics in the group were, if not convinced, at least quieted.

It was near the end of that visit with Chris that he told me something that thrilled me to the core. I was still kind of feeling my way through a conversation with him, via Diane.

"I hope this isn't a rude question, and if I'm not supposed to know, feel free not to answer, but … what is it like on your side of the Veil?"

Diane listened intently, and I could see the other investigators tuning in, too. "He says he gets to be with his family, but he can also come here to the asylum." Then he said something I will never forget.

"When you get to Heaven, I'll be here waiting for you. Just look for the tall skinny guy with dark hair."

Chris was in a delightfully chatty mood when Diane and I visited him in July 2018.

"He says, where have you been, my friend?" Diane said as we walked into the cold storage room.

"Oh, Chris, it's good to see you too! I've been working at the library." Then I muttered to Diane, "Where is he, so I can at least face him when I'm talking to him?"

"He's over by the pillar," Diane assured me. Then she grinned. "He started laughing when you asked where he was."

"Yes, well, you know by now I can't actually see you," I reminded him. "So, Chris, we've just celebrated the Fourth of

July. How did you celebrate Independence Day in your time?"

"He says his family lived out in the country, and on the Fourth, his father would shoot off a gun." He told us that families, neighbors, would get together for a picnic, and the kids would run around and play. "He says it was hot. He wished they'd had a creek." Diane hesitated, then went on. "He says some creeks had leeches in them."

"Yeah, and crawdads." I made a face.

"And snakes," Diane supplied. Then she giggled. "He's laughing at us, saying 'Girls!'" She slipped a bit of teasing disgust into the word.

Still smiling, I told Chris, "I have a couple of surprises for you tonight."

"He says, Yay, surprises! He's just been down here with the grouchy old man."

Again, I didn't even try to explain how I could make sounds come out of the little rectangle of glass and plastic I held in my hand. "Do you remember when Diane and I were here several months ago, and I asked you to hold my hand?"

"He says, it was my pleasure."

I felt heat creep onto my cheeks. I grabbed a chair. "Let's sit down for a while, okay? You can join us, if you want to."

Diane snickered. "He says, you can sit on my lap!"

"Dang, Chris, you are definitely quite the ladies' man, aren't you, even after all this time!" I thought back to our first encounter—not our actual first meeting, but the first time Diane was down there to help us talk to each other. That's when I'd found out how cheeky and friendly Chris actually was. That's also when we'd gotten quite a few EVPs from him. I had another important question for him.

I played one of the EVPs for him, the one that says "*He was 22*".

"Chris, do you know who it was that said this? It doesn't sound like you; it sounds like a woman's voice. Do you know who it was?"

Diane listened for Chris's answer. "He says it might have been one of the patients."

"Can you tell us more?" I pressed. But Diane didn't pick up

anything else for a few long moments.

Then Chris surprised us. "He's talking about Rhoda Derry coming down here. He says, a lady named Rhoda comes down here. She comes to talk with me. He mentions a few times that she comes down, and they talk."

So the speaker on that EVP *could* have been Rhoda. I was so stoked to hear that two of my favorite spirits know each other! I decided it was time to give Chris the next surprise I had planned for him.

"Chris, I taught myself an actual ragtime dance." I hesitated, suddenly shy. I love dancing, but not with a partner. I always feel like a total goober when I try to dance with someone else. "Do you want to dance with me?"

Diane said, "He stood up, and he's holding his hand out to you. I guess he wants to dance!"

Well, I had my answer, and I couldn't very well back out at that point. I took a deep breath, hit PLAY on the recorder on my phone, and walked to the middle of the basement and got ready to dance. With a partner I couldn't see. What was I thinking?

At one point, the Castle Dance calls for both partners to spin. The woman, of course, spins backward. I, of course, spun forward. Because I'm a dork. From across the room, Diane called, "He says you're trying to lead!" To my chagrin, I realized I was doing exactly that.

"Sorry!" I fumbled and reversed. I managed to get through the rest of the dance without any more mishaps. (I hope I didn't step on Chris's toes.) The music stopped, the dance ended, and I breathed a huge sigh of relief.

"Did you like that, Chris?"

"He said you did very well, even though you tried to lead." Diane smiled to take the sting out of her words. "He added, what do you expect? You taught yourself." I didn't get a sense that he was being mean or petty with those words. He was just being … kind, even understanding.

Chris must have asked for another dance at that point, because Diane told him, "She doesn't want to dance any more, she's tired."

"I'm not tired," I corrected her. I turned to Chris. "I'm *not* tired. I'm just a bit embarrassed about mucking up the dance steps! Do you truly seriously want to dance with me again? I'm not all that good of a dancer, as you can tell."

Diane shrugged. "He says, let's dance some more."

So I called up the music for the Castle Dance again, and once more I did my best to stumble gracefully through the steps, being careful to go backwards when the spin came around again. I felt self-conscious, but like a good partner, Chris put me at my ease once the dance was over.

"That was a big joy for him, he says, because he was sick and couldn't go to the dances."

Well of course I just *couldn't* dwell on my clumsy embarrassment then. At least I can dance whenever I feel like it! I sat back down next to the empty chair I had left for him, and invited him to hold my hand again.

I put my hand out, palm down—I usually offer Chris my hand palm up. Immediately I felt warmth on my palm again, a sure physical sign of Chris's attention. Diane quietly translated for him. "Why wouldn't I like holding your hand? You're a pretty lady!" I felt a surge of warmth in my hand. That boy is quite the charmer—no matter that he's been dead for over a century.

As Chris held my hand, we continued our conversation. He confirmed for us that he was at the asylum, suffering from tuberculosis, for a couple of years. (So he did survive the winter of 1905. It's possible he passed sometime during the winter of 1906, but we don't know that for sure.) He spoke of the tent being hot in the summer, and heated by the wood-burning stove in the winter. He said he and the other patients did get to walk around outside in good weather. I marveled aloud that he and I had walked virtually the same ground.

"Yes," Chris replied, "but it looks a lot different now." I could understand that. In my time, the squat brick Pollak Hospital sits on that piece of land. In his time, the white canvas of the tent colony snapped in the passing breeze on the very same spot.

To my delight, Chris remembered the zoo on the grounds. When Dr. Zeller arrived at the asylum to step into his superintendent position, he found the place furnished with all the trappings of a mental institution of that time, which meant grates of metal bars on the windows. Dr. Zeller ordered those grates removed. He refused to make his patients feel like they were living in cages. He took those metal grates and repurposed them into the enclosure for a zoo on the grounds. Chris said it was like a petting zoo, with sheep and goats, and chickens—"lots of chickens".

As we sat chatting, Diane and I kept hearing a soft noise down along the basement walls, like a faint skritching. Diane gave a dainty shudder.

"Ghosts don't bother me, but I don't like mice."

Chris saw his opportunity for another bit of teasing. "A mouse is gonna run up your pants leg!"

I could just picture a school-age Chris sitting behind a girl with long braids, just so he could slyly dip the ends of those braids in the inkwell. We asked him about school. We found out that he didn't go to school regularly. The one room schoolhouse was a long way from where he lived, and sometimes he had to stay home and help with work on his family's farm.

"What did you want to be when you grew up?" I asked. I heard the resigned shrug in Diane's voice as she answered for him.

"Dad said, you're gonna be a farmer. You're going to take over the land, and farm the land."

Chris seemed a bit glum when talking about the duties his father had laid out for him. "Hey, it's not such a bad thing, making things grow," I said. I told him about the fruit and vegetables I raise in my backyard garden.

This seemed to cheer him up. "You sound like a farmer girl!" he kidded.

"Oh no. No no no. I know there's a big difference between farming and gardening."

Chris told us about playing in the corn, and how it would make him itch. He spoke of playing in the barn, and how wild cats would make their homes and have their kittens in the barn. The conversation turned to backyard critters, and he told us how the marauding raccoons would waddle through the fields and eat their corn. Some things don't change, even after a hundred years and more.

"I don't know why I'm the only one," Chris blurted out as our conversation wound down. What did he mean by this? He wouldn't say. Did he mean that he was the only one out of his family able to come back for visits to familiar places? Did he, maybe, mean that he was the only one of his family to die so young? That's a sobering thought ... but again, he refused to elaborate.

He threw in another tidbit about himself, though, just before we left the basement. Out of the blue, Chris shared something with Diane regarding the lost little girl spirit who shares the basement with the other entities. Some of the things Chris says can be a bit cryptic, but this was quite clear.

"The girl doesn't know where to go, so he comes back to see her," Diane said.

They say the good die young ...

So what do we know about Chris, apart from what Diane has been able to share with me? Sadly, not much. I wanted very much to find out more about this friendly, charming young man. I asked him what his last name was. Diane hesitated—she wasn't getting anything from him right away. I said sympathetically, "Has it been that long, that you don't remember?" James Barrow's recorder came up with a soft EVP: "*I remember.*" He finally gave us the last name Pierson, or Peterson. Either way, the last name that he gave us was something that could be spelled half a dozen ways—most of which I tried on both ancestry.com and Find A Grave. Nothing came up. He did tell us that his body had been sent back to his family. They must have been devastated to lose a son and brother so young.

Here's another inescapable heartbreak: Chris probably suffered from some sort of mental illness. The Peoria State Hospital did treat people from the community and surrounding towns for tuberculosis, but only about 10 % of the tuberculosis patients were local. Since Chris was from Indiana, that means his family sent him to the asylum because he was having mental issues. The Peoria State Hospital was famous world-wide for its exemplary care of the mentally ill. It was not a renowned tuberculosis sanatorium, like Waverly Hills. Treatment of tuberculosis was secondary to the treatment of mental illness. (And remember, in those early days the state hospital was still called by its original name, which was the Illinois Asylum for the Incurable Insane, an atrocious name that Dr. Zeller got changed as soon as possible.) So, Chris developed tuberculosis at the asylum, and died here sometime soon after 1905. He was treated for tuberculosis for at least one year, because he has described the tent arrangement in both summer and winter conditions. We have no idea when he got here, or how long he was treated for whatever mental illness brought him to the Peoria State Hospital in the first place.

This presents the question: what was Chris's diagnosis? I have no idea. Diane says that sometimes when she asks him a question, he seems confused, or slow to respond. He doesn't ever seem agitated or dangerous, though. He's told us that he can go back and forth between this plane of existence and the Other Side. I like to think that since he's not an earthbound spirit, maybe whatever issues he had in life have been healed.

All I know is that whenever I visit Chris, I'm charmed all over again. I know he's been dead for well over a century. But Chris seems very much alive to me. (Except, you know, he's invisible.)

And he seems to enjoy my company too. The last time I was down in the basement with Diane, Chris said to me, "Where have you been, my friend?" I asked Diane flat-out where Chris was, so I could face him as I talked, because no, I still can't see him for myself. She said, "He's over there by the pillar. He started laughing when you asked where he was."

If you'd like to experience our conversations with Chris for yourself, I invite you to watch the Lights Out episodes "The Boy in the Basement" (Episode # 55) and "The Boy in the Basement Part 2" (Episode #71) on YouTube, or listen to them on Stitcher, iTunes, or wherever podcasts are heard.

RHODA REVISITED

Without a doubt, Rhoda Derry is the most cherished spirit on the hilltop. Dr. Zeller is revered, Bookbinder remains a source of fascination, but it is Rhoda who brings out a protective sense of empathy in those who hear her story.

The story of Rhoda Derry's life is one of the most horrifying tragedies of mental health care in Illinois, and also one of the most heartwarming success stories of the Peoria State Hospital. Rhoda was born in 1834 and grew up in Adams County, in southern Illinois near Quincy. She was the youngest of nine children, a beautiful girl with long dark hair. She lived in the small town of Lima, and when she was sixteen years old, she met a young man, also sixteen, who lived with his family in the neighboring village of Ursa, less than ten miles away. We don't know how Rhoda met Charles Phenix, but we do know that she did the most natural thing in the world: she fell in love. And when they'd been courting for about two years, Charles asked Rhoda to marry him, and she said yes.

Unfortunately, this was not fated to end in a happily-ever-after for Rhoda. Charles' mother, Nancy Phenix, was rigidly, resolutely against this union. The Derrys were dirt poor. The Phenixes, on the other hand, were rather well off, and Charles was the oldest son of only four children. Nancy Phenix was not about to have her baby boy Charles marry one of these dirt poor Derrys. It was snobbishness, pure and simple, that led Nancy Phenix to confront Rhoda in the street and tell her, "If you do not release my son from this engagement, I will curse you."

Sadly, Rhoda took Nancy's threat seriously. A few weeks after that confrontation, Rhoda had some sort of break with consensual reality. She began to hallucinate that invisible witches were swooping down to attack her. She was sent to the state hospital in Jacksonville, but was released as incurable after two years.

When she returned from Jacksonville, her mental state had not improved. Her family cared for her at home as long as they could, but in 1860, her mother died. Her father could no longer care for her, so he made the agonizing decision to have Rhoda committed to the Adams County Almshouse.

This was about the worst place Rhoda could have ended up. She was very violent—worse yet, she would crawl around on the floor, and anything she found there, a pin, a penny, a nail, she would try to eat it. For her own protection, and because the almshouse staff couldn't watch Rhoda every waking moment, the superintendent of the almshouse decided that Rhoda should be confined in a Utica crib.

A Utica crib is just what it sounds like—it's much like a baby's crib that sits low to the ground, but it also has a barred lid, which locks from the outside. The Utica crib was a common article of furniture in mental asylums and in other places that cared for the mentally ill. But it was never intended for use any longer than overnight. Rhoda was left in her crib for weeks, even months at a time. Think about that for a minute. Just think about it. The people in charge of her care didn't even let her out to go to the bathroom. Instead, they lined the crib with straw to catch some of the waste, and put a tray underneath the crib to keep the rest from falling on the floor. Her hips atrophied from being constantly confined. She soon lost the ability to stand on her own.

Rhoda was in agony. Her fiancé, the love of her life, the man she had planned to spend the rest of her life with, was gone, dust in the wind. She thought she was cursed. Her mother had died. Her father had abandoned her at the almshouse. And now, she was locked in a cage. Sometime during the first ten years of this treatment, Rhoda decided that she no longer wanted to watch the world go by through the bars of a cage, and she clawed her own eyes out. She spent decades in this horrifying situation.

In 1902, Dr. George Zeller became the superintendent of

the Peoria State Hospital. One of his most basic beliefs was that no one was beyond help—no one should ever be considered "incurable". Dr. Zeller set about proving his opinion by visiting the almshouses of Illinois and rescuing the most wretched, abused, mistreated inmates he could find. In September 1904, Dr. Zeller visited the Adams County Almshouse. He found Rhoda there. He rescued her, and he had her brought to the Peoria State Hospital.

Rhoda arrived on the hilltop the night of September 26, 1904. That night, for the first time in forty-four years, she slept in a real bed, with clean white sheets.

Rhoda spent the last two years of her life being waited on hand and foot by attentive, compassionate nurses who knew her excruciating history. She could no longer see, of course, but the nurses made sure that she experienced the hilltop in whatever ways were left to her. They tried to engage all her remaining senses—they let her sit out in the gardens, and feel the warmth of the sun on her face, and listen to the birds singing, and smell the flowers whose colors she could no longer see. They took her to dances, and let her listen to the music.

Rhoda had lost the power of speech sometime during her stay at the almshouse. But she was able to make at least some of her wants known at the Peoria State Hospital. She had picked up the habit of chewing tobacco as a teenager, and in the waning years of her life, she still enjoyed a "chaw". If she knew that a visitor had chewing tobacco in his pocket, she would crab across the floor on her knuckles and knees, then sit and tug on the visitor's pants leg to get his attention, begging silently for a treat.

Rhoda knew without a doubt that Dr. Zeller was her savior, and she adored him for it. Whenever he walked into a room where she was, she lit up, beaming with joyful gratitude. For his part, Dr. Zeller never allowed Rhoda to become just a gruesome curiosity. He invited reporters from all over the country to come to the asylum to see Rhoda, and indeed, many people did come specifically to see her. But Dr. Zeller made sure Rhoda's visitors saw her not as a skeletal scarecrow to be pitied, but as an object lesson in why state hospitals were a necessity.

Rhoda made Dr. Zeller's point for him just by being a patient at the Peoria State Hospital. Rhoda was a living, breathing illustration of how much better a state-funded asylum was than the county-run poor farm that had ruined her life. Dr. Zeller wanted people to realize that the mentally ill did not deserve to be shoved away in almshouses and forgotten, the way Rhoda had been. Rhoda's very survival in the face of such horrific neglect was the most powerful witness to the need to care for the mentally ill in state hospitals, rather than leaving them to the almshouses, which lacked staff trained in the care of such patients.

Rhoda probably developed tuberculosis in the almshouse, and in the summer of 1906 her case became full-blown. She was moved from her cottage into Dining Hall A, which had been pressed into service as a tuberculosis ward. It was there that she passed away on October 9, 1906, the day before she would have celebrated her 72nd birthday.

Rhoda Derry loved the hilltop so much that she started haunting it almost immediately after her passing. She had finally found a place of sanctuary, a place where people cared for her, and cared about her, and she just didn't want to leave. Within weeks of her passing, the staff of Rhoda's cottage on C Row reported seeing a hazy figure hunched on the porch, crouched in Rhoda's accustomed spot.

And her spirit has stayed on the hilltop all these years. Rhoda's tale—her love story with Charles, her conviction that she'd been cursed by Nancy, her decades of hell trapped in a Utica crib, her rescue by Dr. Zeller—is so powerful that it makes a lasting impression on many people who hear it. There are many investigators who have had encounters with Rhoda Derry.

Rhoda loved the hilltop so much that her spirit can be felt anywhere on the asylum grounds. But your best chance of encountering Rhoda is at her gravesite. She is buried in Cemetery One, about half a dozen rows back from the gentle swell of the hill that marks the front of the cemetery. Her grave is always decorated with flowers, remembrances from her many visitors. Two tiny white porcelain cherubs keep silent watch over her resting place.

Rhoda's fondness for chewing tobacco had become an integral part of her ghost lore. If you are anywhere on the hilltop, but especially standing in front of her grave, and you feel a tug on your pants leg and you smell chewing tobacco, that's Rhoda trying to get your attention. James Barrow was at Rhoda's grave one day with another investigator. James turned to his companion and remarked casually that he'd meant to bring some chewing tobacco for Rhoda, but that it had slipped his mind. Moments later, a gravelly voice showed up on his recorder: *"That's okay ... I can't chew any more."*

Another evening, James was paying his respects at Rhoda's grave after a visit to the Pollak Hospital's Haunted Infirmary attraction when his recorder picked up a woman's voice saying, *"James, come on down and sit."* Of course, we have no way of knowing if this spirit voice was actually Rhoda, since she didn't identify herself. But Rhoda seems to be awfully fond of James in particular. It's quite possible that the voice he caught that night was indeed Rhoda, inviting him to "set a spell" on that chilly October evening.

Rhoda has also graced James with a tender observation that he captured during a spirit box session with her. She used the box to have a short conversation with James. In it, she said— wistfully, faintly—*"Yeah, I miss my Charlie."*

James kindly emailed me another story. "I had a run in with her on December 6 while alone on the second floor of the Bowen ... Around the middle of the main corridor I happened to feel a sharp and quite noticeable tug on my left pants leg, and I asked Rhoda if that was her. I didn't hear a response then, but when I played my recorder when I got home, I heard a faint *'It's Rhoda Derry'* before I asked my question. It was followed by a man's and a child's voice, and then Rhoda piped up again saying *'I need a chew.'*"

Here's another example of Rhoda's presence being felt in places on the hilltop that she never visited in life. Rhoda was never in the Employee's Building during her time at the asylum. When she arrived in 1904, she was taken directly from the train station to her cottage. But she seems to have a special bond with

James. Maybe she sought him out in the hallways of the Bowen. I also find it interesting that she announced herself *before* James asked for confirmation that it was indeed her.

Rhoda was never in the Pollak Hospital either, but that doesn't stop her from visiting those hallways as well. I had my own subtle experience with Rhoda in the Women's Ward. I was there with a group of investigators. We weren't getting much activity from the usual suspects, so I told them Rhoda's story to pass the time. Soon after I finished telling the tale, we decided to move to another part of the building, so we made our way out of the Women's Ward.

We had taken maybe half a dozen steps towards the hallway when every single last one of us smelled the distinctive tang of chewing tobacco.

James Barrow has also run into Rhoda at the Pollak Hospital. He was at a Pollak investigation on May 28, 2016, when he decided to poke his head—and his recorder—into one of the exam rooms off the main hallway.

"What's in here ... hello hello?" he called out to any spirits lurking in the room. A naturally curious Pollak spirit gave him his first response. *"Has to be something here."* Then a second EVP came through, and it was a different female voice than the first one.

"I'm right here! Hey kid, it's Rhoda." The EVP is very choppy. The syllables are precisely spit out, one careful sound at a time. It's as if the spirit—Rhoda?—wanted to announce her presence as clearly as she could. 👻

Remember that strange, formal RVP that James caught in the attic of the Bowen, where a spirit claiming to be Rhoda introduced herself to Jerry Zilch? Makes more sense now, doesn't it?

Just because Rhoda grew up in a small town on the Illinois frontier doesn't mean she was a yokel. Rhoda was poor, it's true. But that doesn't mean she didn't possess a quality of poise, of class. It doesn't mean she didn't have manners. Heck, her rough polish may have been the reason Charles Phenix fell in love with her.

There's a Rhoda apparition story I want to share with you. It's going to sound a bit weird, so bear with me. As with everything else I've told you, there's an explanation for the weirdness, I promise.

Christina Morris has seen Rhoda Derry many times, starting when she, Christina, was quite young. The first time Christina saw Rhoda was in the sunken area in front of the Bowen Building that used to be the rose garden. Christina's first sight of Rhoda was utterly unforgettable.

She thought Rhoda was Glinda, the Good Witch.

Let me explain. Christina has pointed out many times that spirits appear to the living according to their own self-image. The way they see themselves is the way they're going to show themselves to you.

Rhoda never saw this hilltop in life. She had blinded herself decades before, sometime during her first ten years in the almshouse. Knowing this, the nurses who cared for her used a stroller or wheelchair to let her experience the hilltop using the senses that were left to her. Rhoda couldn't see her stroller; all she knew was the sensation of rolling.

So sometimes she appears in a big bubble. Not to be too flippant, but I'm told it looks like a big hamster ball. It is *her* conception of the feeling of being rolled to different places on the asylum grounds.

Christina has also seen Rhoda on her deathbed in Dining Hall A. This would be sad enough to witness, just knowing you were seeing a beloved figure of the asylum lying on her deathbed. But Rhoda's apparition in this form is even more unnerving; she has very long arms in proportion to her wasted body. And when she reaches out to someone who can see her … it gets real freaky, real fast.

Rhoda was a tall girl in life. She had long, graceful limbs. But when she was shut up in the Utica crib, her legs became drawn up against her belly as her hips atrophied. This made her long arms even more noticeable. Her hands were grotesquely misshapen too, from using them to propel herself across the floor. It's not her fault she looks so monstrous.

Rhoda's story is very compelling. People who hear it are, quite rightly, appalled at first. *Was she really kept in a cage for forty-four years?* Then the shock turns to gruesome curiosity. *How could anyone claw their own eyes out?*

Unfortunately, there are some people for whom the story ends there. They hear about Rhoda's rescue by Dr. Zeller, but it doesn't really sink in that Rhoda was a real person, a woman with feelings, a woman who loved and suffered and survived.

I'm sorry to say that there are even some ghost hunters that seek out Rhoda just for titillating thrills, and not to show respect for her incredible story. In November 2015, I got a phone call from a television producer in California who wanted to talk about Rhoda Derry. I had done a Halloween interview for a local paper the week before, and the reporter had given the producer my information. The producer and I chatted for a while, and I told her Rhoda's story. Then she asked me to show up at the asylum the following Tuesday evening. They were going to film an episode of Ghost Asylum, with the group Tennessee Wraith Chasers.

Now, I am delighted to share Rhoda's story at every opportunity. It needs to be told. And I have no problem acting as a consultant for people's projects. But Destination America took the information I gave them, and did absolutely nothing with it. As it turned out, the producers chose not to interview me on camera. It's just as well; the episode was riddled with inaccuracies and outright lies. The "historian" they did choose to interview simply fed the ghost hunters the ghoulish haunted asylum stories they were looking for, not any true history.

If you ever happen to watch Episode 3 of Season 3 of Ghost Asylum, please be aware that the entire episode is laughably and lamentably full of disinformation. As far as Rhoda Derry is concerned, looking seriously and exclusively for her spirit in the Bowen Building is an exercise in futility, as she was never there in life.

Here's another thing: Rhoda most certainly did *not* spend her final days "dragging herself around the asylum hallways". That's ridiculous. She spent her final days in the care of compassionate nurses. They treated her like a cherished family member.

And here's what really had me seeing red: Tennessee Wraith Chasers' gimmick is that they build "ghost traps" to attract the spirits of the places they visit. Building a Utica crib to try and trap Rhoda's spirit is utterly despicable. She spent forty-four years of her life in that hell. It represents over four decades of desolate, unimaginable horror. Why would anyone be cruel enough, or stupid enough, to think that Rhoda's spirit would come anywhere *near* that thing? Trying to trap her, and take her away from the place her spirit found peace, is worse than stupid. It's appalling.

Rhoda seems to share our opinion of this episode of Ghost Asylum. Once when James Barrow was recording an EVP session with the intention of communicating with Rhoda, he spoke up about it. He told her about the fiasco that was the Tennessee Wraith Chasers' visit to the Bowen, and he finished with, "So disrespectful!"

Rhoda snapped back, "*I agree!*"

There are a few people who have been fortunate enough to see Rhoda for themselves. And these two sightings, both at the Pollak Hospital, proved to have an important, remarkable similarity.

During the two-day investigation in early July 2016, Lisa Shackelford and Liz Nygard both had encounters with Rhoda Derry. Both women are gifted psychic mediums, powerful and comfortable with their talents.

Lisa Shackelford, lead investigator for Archer Paranormal, was fascinated by Rhoda's story. I shared the tale several times during Friday's hours of investigation, and Lisa pondered it thoroughly. Lisa's group spent some time in the Doll Room on Friday night. Lisa was standing in the room when she felt hands grasping her leg, below the knee. She spoke up and reported it to the group. One of the Pollak guides pointed out that the grabby spirit could well be Rhoda Derry.

"I got chills up and down my spine when she said that," Lisa told me. Lisa describes herself as an intuitive medium. She felt very strongly that she had just been touched by the ghost of Rhoda.

For the rest of that evening, and through the next afternoon, Lisa stewed over the encounter. The touch had led her to brood over Rhoda's fate. "I thought, gosh, it's so unfair! Here she was, she had suffered so horribly all during her life, and now here in the afterlife she's still crawling around on the floor."

But early on Saturday evening, Lisa's intuition was able to set her mind at ease. She was in the hallway of the Pollak, near the entrance hall, getting ready to start the evening's investigation. She became aware that a spirit was crouched on the floor of the hallway. The spirit looked up at Lisa, made eye contact, and smiled. Lisa realized with a start that she was looking at Rhoda Derry.

"In my mind's eye, I saw Rhoda squatting on the floor. But then, she got to her knees, then stood up tall and proud. And she kind of gestured to herself, as if to say, 'See?' That's why she started off crouched on the floor, then stood up. She wanted me to make the connection that it was indeed her spirit I sensed. She tugs on people's legs because that's what they expect to feel from her. She wants people to know it's her. She realizes that people think of her as being blind and crippled. Happily, that's no longer true. She also wants people to know that she is whole, healthy, and sound now. She feels safe and protected here on the hilltop."

Liz Nygard, at that time a member of Shadow Hunters, is an empath from a long line of empaths. Many women in her family, her mother, her grandmother, her great-grandmother, even her daughter, are sensitive to psychic energy. Liz told me with a grin, "I'm basically a walking sonar dish."

Liz is a cheerful, goofy blonde with a penchant for adventurous hats and sequined cats-eye glasses. She was deeply affected by Rhoda's story, to the point where she will not speak Rhoda's name out loud, out of respect. In conversation with me, she prefers to say "Girlfriend down there in the cemetery", or "your girl". Liz assured me that Rhoda has returned to the physical appearance in which she feels most comfortable.

"If you see a proper Victorian lady on the grounds of the

asylum, and you can't quite place her, ask her what her name is," Liz offered.

Easy for her to say, as most of us will not be in a position to *see* a proper Victorian lady ghost anywhere, even on the asylum grounds. "Care to elaborate?" I asked her.

As it turns out, Liz had an encounter with Rhoda in the hallway of the Pollak Hospital, near the front entrance, on the same evening and in almost the same place that Lisa had her experience. Liz told me that Rhoda appeared to her in "shades of blue". Then she shared her experience in greater detail.

"I don't remember Girlfriend speaking. I remember seeing her as she had made herself, severely disabled through hardships and a tortured spirit. I remember her hobbling around within the building, near the piano and the front entrance. I remember her morphing into a proper Victorian woman in fancy garb.

"She has a beautiful crooked smile, and she was able to look at me with very kindly eyes and hold my gaze. Then after her acknowledgement, she was gone. I merely said thank you. I felt honored that she reached out so I could explain it to others. Sometimes nothing spoken says more than anything she could have disclosed."

Something in Liz's story rang a bell in my mind. "Wait ... so basically, she made you aware of her disabilities, then she let you know she was no longer burdened by them—just the same way she did with Lisa?"

"Absolutely," Liz said, "otherwise she would have been just another dead lady. Unless you paired the two together, disability and wholeness, I would not have been able to identify her. The whole thing lasted just a few seconds."

Encounters with Rhoda seem to be very quick like that. But Rhoda's a smart girl. She has figured out a way to let those who see her know that it's *her* they're seeing. She knows her own ghost lore. She knows people expect to feel a tugging on their pants leg when she's around, so that's what she does. And for those lucky people who are sensitive enough to actually see her, she reveals herself to be the tall, beautiful, spirited young lady she once was, when she was being courted by Charles Phenix.

Rhoda Derry deserves to spend eternity young and beautiful.

THE LADY IN WHITE

One of my favorite ghost tropes is the tale of the Lady in White (or the Lady in Pink, or the Blue Lady, or the Gray Lady—take your pick). The White Lady is practically standard issue for haunted theaters, castles, manor houses, and the like. She drifts from place to place, sometimes spooking the unsuspecting passerby, most of the time just minding her own business. She can be a mother mourning her lost children, a maiden mourning her lost love, or just a wandering female spirit. All the *best* haunted places have a White Lady.

Here at the Peoria State Hospital, we have at least three, and possibly as many as half a dozen.

When the asylum opened on February 10, 1902, it started off with one hundred patients from the Illinois State Hospital in Jacksonville. The asylum took in the most challenging cases from the other state hospitals. Dr. Zeller, of course, wanted to rescue patients from where they languished in almshouses, which he eventually did. The population swelled quickly—by June 30 of that year, there were 622 patients in residence. On June 30, 1903, there were 698 residents, and on June 30, 1904, 762 patients called the asylum home.

This rapid influx of patients soon overwhelmed the cottages in A Row and B Row, and Dr. Zeller and the asylum board soon realized that there was a desperate need for more housing. Construction began on the C Row cottages.

Meanwhile, the trains kept on bringing more patients in need of help. And Dr. Zeller and his staff kept on welcoming these patients. But where to put them?

Dr. Zeller knew that physical activity was a good antidote to mental illness. Where possible, he found things for his patients to do. This kept them occupied, and hopefully, got them out of their own heads for a while each day. As a bonus, it helped with the day to day running of the institution.

The men who were building the cottages were already being put up in the general storehouse while they worked. Since able-bodied male patients were helping with these tasks, Dr. Zeller decided to house them with the other workers. One hundred and fifty male patients lived in the general storehouse for almost three years.

And what about the women? Female patients arrived on the hilltop with needs just as pressing as those of the male patients. They were put up in the Employee's Building, the structure that later became known as the Bowen Building. For about nine months, student nurses lived alongside 128 criminally insane women.

Yes, I heard your gasp all the way over here. When I call these women "criminally insane", you might assume they were violent. This wasn't necessarily the case. Throughout the nineteenth century, and even into the early days of the twentieth century, you didn't go to a psychiatrist or a counselor if you were having mental troubles. Instead, your family members or other concerned people brought you into court. It was a judge, not a doctor, who decided whether or not you should be put into an asylum.

Many of these women were hauled into court, not by concerned relatives fearing insanity, but by the police officers who had arrested them. These were women who, for one reason or another, ended up in jail. They may have been battered women who fought back against their abusers. They may have been suffering from postpartum depression and tried to harm their children. They may have been arrested for petty theft, for stealing food or riding a trolley without paying the fare. For whatever reason, they found themselves in court, facing a judge.

Dr. Zeller knew of this. He worked in the Peoria court system. He knew these women were often sent to prison. And if they were also suffering from mental illness, prison was *not* the place for them. Sending someone with mental problems to languish in prison was virtually a death sentence.

Dr. Zeller had a lot of compassion for all his patients, but he felt especially tenderly towards women. He visited the courtrooms of Peoria on a regular basis. Whenever a judge was about to sentence a woman to jail, Dr. Zeller would step in. He'd suggest that the woman be sent to his asylum instead. He saved lives this way.

The upshot of all of this was that for about nine months, from the late spring of 1903 to the early spring of 1904, 128 female patients lived with the nurses in the Employee's Building. This was a temporary arrangement, of course. It was never designed to be otherwise. These women, and their children, were the first patients to move into the C Row cottages when they were completed in the spring of 1904.

So what does all this have to do with our Lady in White?

Well, she was most often seen in the hallways of the Bowen Building.

In fact, there are several candidates for the title of White Lady, out of the spirits that used to wander the halls of the Bowen. She could have been a nurse (although no nurse ever died in the Bowen). She could have been one of those criminally insane women (although none of them ever died in the Bowen either).

She could have been Anne M. Stuart, a housekeeper for the student nurses' dorm. On October 4, 1915, she took ill while going about her duties. She was taken to her room to recover, but she slipped into a diabetic coma and faded quickly. She died the very next evening. It is the housekeeper's spirit that used to haunt the attic of the Bowen. She could be heard bustling around, straightening bedclothes and tidying up living quarters long gone. Sometimes, she would sing "Ave Maria" quietly to herself.

Anne Stuart is certainly a good possibility for the Lady in White. She was a dedicated employee, and loved her job, enough to stay on after her death. In the Biennial Report for 1916, Superintendent Ralph Hinton praised Stuart, saying that "she entered upon her duties with much enthusiasm … the day was never too long, her work never too arduous ... She seemed to tire easily, but with it all never complained." She even, Hinton noted, came to work early on the day she fell ill.

But at the top of the shortlist for potential Ladies in White in the Bowen Building is Sophie Zeller herself.

The iconic sighting of the Lady in White, at least at the Bowen, was of a graceful phantom in a flowing white dress going down a hallway. This specter had a confident attitude—she gave off an air of self-importance, of strong self-esteem, of being exactly where she wanted to be. (In fact, she intimidated some of the people who saw her. Instead of seeing her as self-confident, they misinterpreted her forceful presence as threatening.)

This prepossessing sense of self describes Sophie Zeller right down to the ground. She was the perfect partner for George. They never had children; they considered the patients of the asylum their children. (Just as an aside, there may be a perfectly valid reason why the couple never had kids. They got married in 1889, when George was 31 years old—fairly late for marriage, especially for that time. George was busy trying to establish his medical practice. He was utterly devoted to Sophie, and she to him, but marriage seems to have been pretty low on his list of priorities. For her part, it's possible that in her younger years, Sophie contracted mumps or scarlet fever or some other ailment, something that was not fatal, but stole her ability to bear children.)

We know from newspaper articles that at the end of her life, Sophie Zeller languished with some kind of illness for two years. During this time, she and George lived in an apartment on the second floor of the Bowen Building. Sophie loved the asylum, and the Employee's Building, just as much as George did. And why not? She was devoted to George, and so was everyone else. The staff of the asylum treated her husband with the utmost respect. They named him Superintendent Emeritus upon his retirement, and invited the couple to spend the rest of their lives in the apartment in the Employee's Building. (For that story, please see the chapter on the Bowen.) And the patients of the asylum adored him. It was often said that Dr. Zeller was a military man to his employees, and a father figure to his patients. And Sophie was their mother figure. Sophie was George's staunch partner throughout their marriage.

Sophie and George Zeller

Sophie spent her last two years just as George did, surrounded by nurses who cared for her with real kindness and love. She died in October 1937 in the Bowen Building. George would follow her several months later, in June 1938.

Sophie Zeller is the perfect example of a spirit who haunts a place because they loved it in life. If we cast Sophie in the role of the Lady in White, we see a spirit who sees herself as important, as *integral* to the functioning of the asylum. We know this to be true about Sophie. We see a spirit with a powerful sense of self-confidence, which also fits Sophie's personality in life. We can even go a little further, if we want to, and say that the regal spirit inspires respect in some of those who see her.

And that, most certainly, describes Sophie Zeller.

One more interesting thing to note about the Lady in White who hung around the Bowen: this phantom was seen most often in the hallways of the building, but was also seen on the road next to the building. Here's what's intriguing—when Pfeiffer Road was extended in the early 1980s, the porch that wrapped around the side of the building was removed to accommodate the road. So this spirit is basically still hanging out on a porch that no longer exists. And this story, of the White Lady at the Bowen being seen in the road, started to gain traction around 1983 when the road was extended.

Sadly, Sophie's spirit isn't felt as often now that the Bowen has come down. There was, at one time, a gorgeous rose garden in front of the Bowen, a garden of which Sophie was very proud. It's possible that the rose garden drew her spirit to the Bowen after she passed, and formed a focus for her presence there. She was proud of the Bowen too, and of the asylum that her husband worked so hard to make a place of refuge and security. She loved the institution, she loved George, and she loved the good work they were doing together. Now that the Bowen and so many other buildings are gone, now that the roses no longer bloom, Sophie's presence seems to have faded from the hilltop.

Speaking of phantoms who are seen in the road, we do have two more spirits in the running for the title of the Lady in White. As you come up the hill from Route 29, Pfeiffer Road curves gently and deposits you in the heart of the asylum grounds. But that part of Pfeiffer Road didn't exist when the asylum was a going concern.

When the Peoria State Hospital was open, the Levitin and Talcott Hospitals served the patients who needed medical care. The Levitin, named for Emil Levitin, was for female patients, and the Talcott, named for Mary Bird Talcott, was for male patients.

Surgeries were performed in the basement of each hospital.

When Pfeiffer Road was extended down to Route 29 in the early 1980s, the hospitals were torn down, joining the roll call of buildings that were demolished around that time. So when you turn to go up the hill, you are actually driving through a space that used to be the basement of the Levitin.

Where surgeries were performed.

And sometimes, patients don't survive surgery.

See where I'm going with this?

There have been drivers who have reported seeing a female figure in a white robe standing in the road in that area. This phantom might very well be a female patient from the Talcott who didn't make it through her surgery, or died in spite of surgical treatment.

Then again, this particular Lady in White may be someone else entirely … another patient, as it turns out.

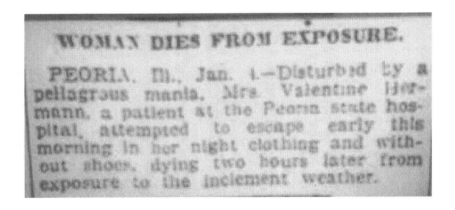

WOMAN DIES FROM EXPOSURE.

PEORIA. Ill., Jan. 4.—Disturbed by a pellagrous mania. Mrs. Valentine Hermann, a patient at the Peoria state hospital, attempted to escape early this morning in her night clothing and without shoes, dying two hours later from exposure to the inclement weather.

Vitamin deficiencies can wreak serious havoc on the human body. One of the worst of these is pellagra, which is caused by low levels of niacin (vitamin B3). Pellagra was epidemic at the Peoria State Hospital in 1909, due to the patients' diet being based too much on corn and cornmeal. Dr. Zeller cut back on the amount of corn products on the menu, and by 1911, the epidemic had largely subsided. It still killed a staggering number of people: of the 258 patients who suffered with pellagra between 1908 and 1911, 128 of them died.

Pellagra is a deeply unpleasant disease. Among other indignities, like diarrhea and blackened skin on the face, hands, and feet, pellagra also causes dementia. A patient, Valentine Hellman, was one of the patients stricken in the most serious outbreak of the disease at the asylum. On January 4, 1910, caught in the grip of mania, she wandered away from her cottage without shoes and dressed only in her nightgown. Two hours later, she was found frozen to death in one of the ravines. Two nurses were charged with negligence for failing to realize that Valentine had wandered off. They were found guilty and lost their jobs.

Does Valentine still haunt the ravine where she died, and occasionally drift into the road that runs next to the ravine, still wearing her white nightgown? And if so, is she still battling the mania of pellagra? Or does she suffer guilt over the two nurses losing their livelihood because of her, after providing such compassionate care?

Whether this particular Lady in White is a patient who didn't survive surgery, or the ill-fated Valentine, one thing is for sure: she is still seen. And this White Lady, who appears at the crest of the hill on Pfeiffer Road, has an aspect that is markedly different to the White Lady further up the road at the Bowen Building. The Bowen White Lady wears a long, flowing white gown, and is seen close to the Bowen, hardly on the road at all. The crest-of-the-hill White Lady is dressed in white too, but it's a spare hospital johnny, the garb of a patient. They are obviously two different apparitions.

Sylvia Shults

Ladies in white photo

This photograph, staged for the camera, represents one of our possible Ladies in White.

The Peoria State Hospital is home to many kinds of ghosts, from residual hauntings to intelligent spirits. The hilltop rivals any drafty European castle or Civil War battlefield for the sheer density of its spectral population.

And yes, we have our own Lady in White.

THE TRAVELING NURSE

Springfield, Illinois, is the home base of a wonderful group called Prairieland Paranormal Consortium. They meet once a month at a local community college to discuss—well, anything paranormal. Ghosts, astral projection, Sasquatch, spiritual protection, UFOs ... anything is fair game for serious discussion. The group is all-inclusive in their search for knowledge, which is why it is such a joy to attend one of their meetings. As soon as you walk through the classroom door, you can sense the open-minded curiosity that draws these folks together.

A few years ago, I was invited by Carl Jones, the facilitator for Prairieland Paranormal Consortium, to give a talk on the history and hauntings at the Peoria State Hospital. (For those of you interested in synchronicity, here's one for you: I was the first speaker that afternoon, and unbeknownst to me, the "second act" was Brandon Lamprecht, the filmmaker who did a short film about Bookbinder and was then working on a feature film about Rhoda Derry. We got to talking after his presentation, and he suggested I write a book about Rhoda. That was the day *44 Years in Darkness* was born.)

I gave my talk, and then I settled down to watch "Bookbinder" and the teaser trailers for "The Mysterious Rhoda Derry". I found myself sitting next to a lovely woman, whose name I unfortunately cannot remember. We got to chatting, and agreed that the films we'd just watched were a fascinating look at a couple of asylum residents. She told me that she'd enjoyed my talk, too, and I thanked her. Then she said something that rocked my world.

"Do you know you have a nurse that follows you around?"

I blinked. "No, I had no idea."

The lady gave me a sweetly tolerant smile. "Oh yes, she shows up every time you do a talk on the asylum, and she stands a little ways behind you. She's dressed in an old-fashioned nurse's uniform, with a neat white apron. She says that the asylum staff is so proud of you for sharing the hospital's history, and she says that everyone on the Other Side is 'all atwitter' that they're in a book."

I smiled as her words sank in. How amazing to have my own supernatural cheering section! I thanked her again for telling me about the nurse. Later, as I chatted with Carl Jones, I mentioned what the woman had shared with me. Carl's eyes grew wide.

"Oh, Sylvia, she is a gifted medium, very gifted. She does paranormal investigations, too. And sometimes, she finds out she'd going on an investigation on Saturday because on Wednesday or Thursday, spirits will come to her and say, 'You're going to be at my house on Saturday—here's what I want you to know.' If she tells you that you have a nurse who follows you, that's exactly what's going on."

Carl's words, and those of the medium, proved to be entirely true. About a year or so later, I was a speaker at the Chicago Ghost Con, and my talk was, again, on the Peoria State Hospital. Before I was scheduled to speak, I was at my table, which happened to be next to that of another psychic medium. We struck up a conversation, and she mentioned that there was a nurse standing next to me.

"She gets a bit irritated with you sometimes," the psychic told me, "because you don't acknowledge her."

"That's only because I don't know she's there!" I yelped. "It's not that I'm not delighted she shows up—I'm thrilled. But I can't see or hear her when she's around. I'm sorry!"

The nurse must have heard my outburst, because ever since then, she has made her presence clear … if I don't say something about her at the beginning of my talks, she lets me know, gently but firmly, that she is less than pleased.

It started, appropriately enough, at another Prairieland Paranormal Consortium meeting. I had a thing to go to in

Jacksonville that evening, so I stopped in at the college on my way down. It was an impromptu visit, but Carl talked me into doing the asylum presentation while I was there (admittedly, not a hard sell for me). I guess the nurse was a bit salty with me for not greeting her at the place where we'd originally "met", because the laptop kept advancing the slides for the talk when I was nowhere near it.

I soon realized that if I wanted the projector and laptop to function smoothly at an asylum talk, I needed to say something at the beginning of the talk to let the audience know the nurse was there. It doesn't take very long, and the simple act of acknowledging the nurse's presence seems to keep her happy. I think she has come to accept, by now, the fact that I can't see her, much as I would like to.

I gave a talk at the Bloomington Public Library, and mentioned my nurse. A friend of mine, Laura Kennedy, came up to me after the talk and told me that when I explained about the nurse, she could see a small faint glimmer of light fluttering joyfully behind me. "I thought it was a moth," she said, "but now I think it might have been your nurse."

I'll admit, sometimes I forget to give my familiar shout-out, especially if it's been a while between performances. But when I forget, she kindly reminds me. The month of October 2018 was quite busy for me, with talks twice a week for much of the month. I spoke at Lillie M. Evans Library on a Tuesday night, and neglected to mention my nurse. The projector just ... stopped. Black screen, no one could figure out why. But I knew why. I apologized to the nurse, then turned to the audience and explained that yes, I had a nurse who came to every one of my asylum talks, and yes, I really should have taken a moment and introduced her to the audience. Moments later, the projector clicked to life, and I went on with my presentation.

Two days later, on Thursday night, I was at the Mackinaw Library for a talk. It's a small library, and their equipment is decidedly not state of the art. The librarian warned me that their projector could be a bit balky at times. I explained that if I welcomed the nurse to the talk, we'd have no technical problems that evening.

And we didn't.

My nurse still faithfully shows up every time I give a presentation on the Peoria State Hospital, just as the psychic told me years ago. Last year, Dale Kaczmarek asked me to fill in for another speaker at the last minute, at an event being held at the Evangelical Spiritual Church in Cicero, Illinois. Dale specifically asked me to speak on the asylum. "That's my favorite of your talks," he told me, and I was delighted to share the history and hauntings of the hilltop.

As the venue was a Spiritualist church, I was pretty confident that someone in the audience would actually be able to see my nurse. So as soon as I got on stage, I let the audience know that if anyone should see a nurse in an old-fashioned uniform standing behind me, yes, she was from the Peoria State Hospital, and yes, she was definitely with me.

Later that afternoon, someone came by my table to chat. She told me that she had, indeed, seen my nurse standing on stage with me. And this time, she had a message for me.

"She says, stand up straight, and stop second-guessing yourself."

BOOKBINDER—THE TRUE STORY

Every Halloween, in the Peoria area, local newspapers delight in retelling the oldest ghost story on the hilltop—the tale of Bookbinder.

Early on, a patient was brought to the Peoria State Hospital because he'd had a nervous breakdown at work. His breakdown was so total that he was rendered mute, unable to tell the intake nurses his name. He came to Bartonville from the Chicago Asylum, and they could provide very little information on him. All anyone knew about him was that he had worked in a factory, binding books. His name, therefore, was written down in the intake ledger as A. Manual Bookbinder. He became known familiarly as "Old Book".

Bookbinder was encouraged, as were all the able-bodied inmates, to find useful work to do at the asylum to keep his mind and body occupied. It became Book's duty to care for the cemeteries on the hilltop. This included grave digging detail.

At the first funeral Book attended, he was standing next to the grave, and his shoulders began to hitch. Tears leaked from his eyes and tracked silently down his cheeks. A sob escaped him, and he walked over to the large elm tree that stood in the middle of the cemetery. There, he leaned against the trunk of the tree and wailed, crying as if his heart was breaking. When the short service was over, he collected himself and came back to fill in the grave.

Old Book did this at every funeral he attended, and he attended every funeral that was held on the hilltop. Once, when he was ill, he saw a hearse passing by, with a body that was destined to be put on the train to be returned to a family for burial in a family plot. Book became quite agitated at the thought that he might be missing the chance to wail at a funeral, and Dr. Zeller had to quickly assure him that the body was headed elsewhere, and not to a hilltop grave. Old Book became such a fixture at asylum funerals that he became an urban legend of sorts. If a patient felt that they were on their deathbed, they would snag a passing nurse and request, "Please make sure Old Book cries for me, or else I won't get into Heaven."

In 1910, Old Book himself passed away. (He may have died of tuberculosis, but there was also a pellagra epidemic raging through the asylum at the time, so that may have been the cause of his death.) Old Book was a well-known and well-loved character at the asylum, so his funeral was very well attended.

What happened next comes to us from the memoirs of Dr. Zeller himself. He said that the mourners had just finished singing Rock of Ages, and were preparing to lower Book's coffin into the grave. Four men grabbed the ends of the ropes that were slung under the coffin, and heaved to lift it so the boards underneath could be slid out. The coffin, though, bounced up into the air as if it weighed no more than an eggshell.

And just at that moment, everyone in attendance heard a wailing and crying coming from the Graveyard Elm. They turned in horror to look—and there was the ghost of Old Book, leaning against the tree in his accustomed place, moaning and carrying on as if his heart was breaking.

Astonished nurses fell to their knees, or scrambled to get away. Dr. Zeller ordered the coffin opened. Someone grabbed a crowbar and jimmied the lid off. As soon as the coffin lid was raised, the wailing stopped, the phantom vanished—and there lay Old Book, in his coffin. He was undeniably dead. Dr. Zeller wrote, "It was awful, but it was real. I saw it. One hundred nurses and three hundred spectators saw it."

The story of Old Book doesn't end there. After about six weeks, the old elm tree started to die. Workers poured buckets of water on it—no one wanted to see Old Book's tree go—but the tree kept on dropping leaves, and soon it was obvious that the tree was dying. Dr. Zeller was a very safety-conscious guy, he didn't want a limb coming down and injuring someone, so he sent a work crew out to chop the tree down.

The crew came back less than an hour later, with a terrifying tale. They said that at the first stroke of the axe, they'd heard a wailing coming from the trunk of the old elm—a wailing that sounded a lot like the voice of Old Book.

Dr. Zeller sent out a fire crew to burn the tree down. The crew piled kindling around the dying tree's trunk, poured a bit of kerosene on it to get it going, and touched the match to it. But in the smoke that began to curl up, they swore they saw the face of Old Book, drawn with sadness. And in the crackling of the flames, they heard Book's sorrowful cries. They threw water on the flames and came running back to Dr. Zeller, saying they didn't want any part of destroying Book's tree.

So the old tree was allowed to die on its own. And legend has it that when the tree did finally fall, it fell right between the rows of gravestones, and didn't damage a single stone as it fell. Groundskeepers rolled the carcass of the big tree into the ravine that borders Cemetery Two, where it returned to the earth, just as Old Book had done.

Is it a good story? Oh, you bet. It has drama, tears, terror, a satisfyingly spooky denouement.

Is it true?

Well … no.

Dr. Zeller was an accomplished writer of short stories. He became known as "the Rudyard Kipling of America" for the quality of his work, and Rudyard Kipling—the original—wrote to him, complimenting him on his tales. Dr. Zeller found a wealth of story ideas in the people he saw every day, and he honored the people in his care by telling their stories.

And sometimes, he embellished the facts.

Dr. Zeller was so taken by Bookbinder's devotion to his job that he knew he had to immortalize him in print. The spook story of the weeping gravedigger soon took on a life of its own. Dr. Zeller began to receive letters from the superintendents of other institutions, letters that betrayed a bit more than professional curiosity. The other asylum heads were dying to know … they'd been hearing some nutty story about a ghost crying at his own funeral, and they just had to know, was it true? Dr. Zeller would get this question fairly often as he travelled to visit his colleagues at other hospitals. He finally decided to come clean.

He wrote a blanket letter to the psychiatric journals to which he was a contributor. (In the days before emails and forums, this was as good—and efficient—as it got.) A copy of this letter even appeared in the venerable Journal for Psychical Research, begun in England in 1884 for the purpose of examining the inexplicable in a scientific spirit. So people were definitely getting into the weirdness of the story, even though it had been reported by a well-respected state hospital superintendent. A former member of the Peoria State Hospital Museum, Jillian Wallace, found the letter in the records of the asylum in the course of her research.

In this letter, Dr. Zeller basically 'fessed up. The gist of the letter was simple: we have a lot of really good folks in our asylum. Some of them are what you'd call "real characters". And yes, some of them make it into my fiction writing.

So what's the takeaway from Dr. Zeller's confession?

Let's look again at the history. Was there a patient at the asylum named "A. Manual Bookbinder", who went by the nickname "Old Book"? Yes, there was. Was he assigned to graveyard duty? Yes, he was. Did he cry at every funeral? Yes, he did. Dr. Zeller saw this, and he was inspired by Bookbinder's compassion. The only thing that bothered him was that when Bookbinder was gone, there would be no one to weep as unabashedly for him as he had wept for others.

So Dr. Zeller made it happen.

GRACE ABBOTT CHILDREN'S CENTER

James Barrow, an investigator with Spirits in the Night, has a deep passion for the Peoria State Hospital. As often as he can, he will explore the Pollak Hospital, or simply wander the hilltop, recorder at the ready, hoping to catch a stray snippet of a ghostly voice.

One March day in 2015, he decided to do a little experiment. He went to the library.

The building that eventually became the Grace Abbott Children's Center began life as the dairy barn in 1902. Farm Colony Two supplied fresh milk to the asylum's main campus one and a half miles away. By 1951, the asylum was getting its milk from the community, so the dairy barn was no longer needed.

There were children at the state hospital for the asylum's entire history. The children who were there as patients ranged in age from five to twenty years old. (Technically, Christopher may have fallen into this age range. He passed when he was twenty-two, but we don't know how long he'd been at the asylum before he died. He could very well have been admitted to the hospital before the age of twenty.)

Early state hospital records show two deaths of patients under age twenty for the period 1903 to 1906. And in the Eighth Biennial Report, published in 1910, the youngest patient on the hilltop for that year is listed as an eleven year old girl.

In the early 1950s, there was a growing awareness in the psychiatric community regarding the specific needs of mentally ill children. The Peoria State Hospital didn't waste any time seeing to the needs of some of their most vulnerable patients. The old dairy barn was refurbished into a 36-bed facility, and on October 8, 1951, it was opened as the Grace Abbott Children's Center. The building was named for Grace Abbott, who began her career at Hull House in Chicago, and became a leader in the field of social work devoted to children.

The center served prepsychotic and psychotic children ranging from six to fourteen years of age. The Abbott Center program was unique in the state, and soon it received national accreditation. The center soon outgrew the former dairy barn, and a Quonset building was put up that held two classrooms and a gymnasium. The center also boasted a library and a riding stable, with four horses and their tack donated by local citizens. A two-acre lake was stocked with fish, and also provided opportunities for boating and swimming.

Celebrities were brought in specifically for the kids at Abbott Center. In fact, the volunteer program at the Peoria State Hospital was primarily developed to bring entertainment to the children at Grace Abbott. These celebrity guests included puppeteer Fran Allison (of the TV show *Kukla, Fran, and Ollie* which aired in the late 1940s and early 1950s); actor Duncan Rinaldo, popularly known as "The Cisco Kid"; baseball greats Curt Flood and Stan Musial; and performers from the Arthur Murray Dance Studio. In 1958, activities expanded even further, with field trips to Peoria, picnics, and swimming at the YWCA.

In 1959, Boy Scout Troop 241 was established at the center. Previously, boys had belonged to troops in Bartonville. Now they had their own charter—something that was absolutely unique in mental hospitals.

(As a matter of fact, the boys in the troop were privileged to have one of the earliest paranormal experiences on the hilltop, not counting the fable of Bookbinder. This happened even before the asylum closed. Bill Turner, Activity Therapy employee at the asylum, would sometimes take the boys out at night for astronomy lessons. One evening as the group was headed out for a night of stargazing, their hike took them through Cemetery Three-Four. The boys swore they could see a shadow figure darting between the gravestones.)

1964 brought even more opportunities for the children at

Grace Abbott. They enjoyed periodic shopping trips and physical education classes. A playroom was set up for the younger children, with dozens of well-dressed dolls to populate it. A volunteer program was developed to give the adolescent boys experience in socializing with girls their own age.

Unfortunately, the children's program was one of the first on the chopping block in Peoria State Hospital's phaseout. On September 18, 1967, eight children were transferred to the children's unit of Zeller Zone Center in Peoria. The remaining four kids were transferred to treatment facilities in their home communities, or discharged. After sixteen years in operation, Grace Abbott Children's Center was closed.

So what does this have to do with James Barrow's field trip to the library? Well, about five years after the Abbott Center closed, the village of Bartonville got its first library. The board decided to call it Alpha Park Library, after the first letter of the Greek alphabet. (First letter, first library—get it?) In 1972, the Abbott Center opened its doors once again, and became the original Alpha Park Library.

James's theory was this: why not try to capture some EVPs in the present library building? Sure, the library left the Abbott Center Building in 1985 when the new library was built, just across Airport Road from the old place. But maybe a few spirits decided to make the move to the new building. Also, the land on which the present library sits would have been the playground for the Abbott Center. To find out, James went undercover.

He started by asking a librarian for help in finding some books on the paranormal—a great cover story, in my opinion. As he followed the librarian to the correct shelf, he was also surreptitiously listening to a spirit box through his earbuds. James knew they would pass some Peoria State Hospital relics on the way to the stacks—Dr. Zeller's office furniture, various pieces of old medical equipment, early Peoria State Hospital nursing school class pictures. He was hoping the voices would pipe up as they passed this memorabilia.

"As the librarian was leaving after she showed me the right shelf, my recorder caught a voice that seemed … well … off.

I wasn't sure if it was the librarian saying something as she walked away, or if it was a spirit."

The voice said, *"You can find what you need in here."*

Two minutes later, James caught another voice. Even though he was still listening to the spirit box, he felt it sounded like an EVP rather than an RVP (radio voice phenomenon). *"You got to help! Help me."*

After about half an hour of browsing the stacks, James found a secluded study spot tucked into a corner. He settled in, pretending to be nothing more than a library patron listening to a bit of music while he enjoyed a book. In reality, though, James's spirit box was steadily sweeping the radio dial, searching for any snippets of sound that might be the voices of the dead.

James felt comfortable enough by now to ask a few questions in a low voice. "Any spirits here from Grace Abbott Center or Peoria State Hospital?"

"There's several ... spirits."

"Hello, James."

Encouraged by the responses, James continued. "This used to be the children's ward of the old place. Are any of the children still here?"

A male voice replied, *"Probably."* Then a young boy's voice chimed in, *"Me!"*

James kept the recorder and spirit box going as he walked through the library on his way out. In the middle of the room, he caught a spirit voice that sounded like a preteen boy. The voice lilted, *"Hello! ... I'm Eric."*

Then James was delighted to hear a happy yelp from the spirit box. *"James ... I found ya!"* James seems to have a special relationship with the spirits that are associated with the Bowen Building. Even though the building has been demolished, the spirits are still there. James's theory is that perhaps, as he drove past the site of the Bowen on his way to the library, one of the spirits saw him and followed him across town.

I spoke with John Richmond, the director of Alpha Park Library, about the library's history. We had previously met in a professional setting, at a couple of library conferences, so he welcomed me into his office. I shifted in my chair, hoping I wouldn't destroy his professional opinion of me with my questions.

"So," I began, "did anyone, staff, patrons, ever have any paranormal experiences in the old building?"

John gave me a genuine smile and shook his head. "No, that just wasn't part of the lore." He told me that the attic of the building was used for storage, and that as far as he knew, no one ever reported ghostly footsteps up there, or anything paranormal at all. (I also spoke with MarySue Baker, who started out as a page at the old building, and retired from the new building a few years ago. She said that they used to store the Reader's Guide to Periodicals, a huge series of green-covered reference books that listed all of the articles in all of the magazines published each year, up in the attic of the old building. When the pages would go up there to retrieve the Reader's Guide for a patron, the attic would be freezing cold ... but just in the winter, when it would be expected. She never gave me any sense that anything paranormal happened in the building.)

"The old building was used by as many groups of people that wanted to use it," John told me. I got the impression that the old dairy barn served the community of Bartonville well, in all its incarnations. There was a soft note of regret in John's voice as we came to the end of our conversation.

"It was sad to see that building come down."

MYSTERIOUS DEATHS AND MURDERS

"DYNAMITE Was Used By The Aged Madman To Blow His Head From His Body.

"*Special dispatch to The Enquirer:* Peoria, Ill., August 15 (1909).—Charles P. Jones, aged 73, whose home is at Hanna City, Ill., blew his head off with a dynamite cartridge in a ravine near the Peoria State Hospital for the Insane to-day.

"Jones was admitted to the asylum August 3 on his own request. His case was but a mild one and he chatted cheerfully with the nurses a few nights before he committed his rash act. He had the freedom of the grounds and doubtless got the dynamite cartridge from a near-by coal mine.

"The blast severed his head from the body as if done by a guillotine, and while nothing could be found of the head, the body was in good shape."

Because of the no-locked-door policy at the asylum, patients were free to wander the grounds. Jones seems to have discovered one of the old coal mines that were worked in that area in the mid-nineteenth century.

Contrary to what you might think, dynamite is relatively stable. It needs something to set it off. This is what blasting caps are for. A blasting cap is a small device about the size and shape of a hockey puck. Inside it are two wires, one coming in from each end, and a bunch of an explosive called mercury fulminate, which is highly unstable. When the two ends of the wires touch inside the cap, they make a spark, which sets off the mercury fulminate. That makes a shock wave which detonates the dynamite.

One of these blasting caps was inadvertently left behind at a mine. Jones found it, pocketed it, and found a sad, final use for it. As far as anyone can tell, he put the blasting cap in his mouth, then bit down (or shoved his jaw closed with the heel of his hand). I say "as far as anyone can tell", because they never found any part of his head. It had been blown to bits.

With all our discussion of the hauntings at the Peoria State Hospital, we can't—and we shouldn't—lose sight of the fact that this was a place where the mentally ill came for help. The asylum was incredibly good at this—it had the highest rate of reintegration into society of any institution in the country. But sometimes, patients' demons were just too powerful. Sometimes, patients could no longer fight against their problems.

And these patients, too, ended up staying on the hilltop. The fellow who used a blasting cap for a decidedly off-label purpose is one of those spirits. As a matter of fact, you may have seen him on TV.

When the TAPS crew came to the Peoria State Hospital in 2012 to investigate the Bowen Building, they took a field trip over to the next block and explored Cemetery Two. Britt and KJ set up a battery powered, self-contained full spectrum camera in the cemetery. A full spectrum camera captures images in wavelengths beyond what our eyes can see—hence the name.

Bookbinder, of course, is the most famous patient buried in this cemetery. So when the camera caught a dark figure at the tree line next to the ravine, everyone assumed that the ghost hunters must have scared up Bookbinder. It's obvious, right? If you see a ghost in Cemetery Two, it must be Old Book.

But! Remember that Bookbinder's ghost was actually made up by Dr. Zeller. Much as we'd love to claim that Old Book still roams the cemetery as he did in life, it's just ... I'm sorry ... it's just not true. Dr. Zeller even admitted it.

So if Old Book isn't wandering around in the ravine next to Cemetery Two ... who is?

Well, keep in mind that our fellow who went out with a bang did the deed in one of the ravines. If anyone would be haunting the ravines after such an explosive exit, it would be this guy.

(And if it makes you feel any better, consider this: since Jones killed himself in 1909, and since Bookbinder was here from 1906 to 1910 and attended every funeral, it's almost a certainty that Old Book buried Jones. So there is a connection between the two men.)

When it comes to the paranormal, some thoughtful, informed detective work can often go a long way towards solving a mystery. Christina Morris likes to tell the story of an EVP she accidentally captured years ago.

Christina and a few other people were investigating in the Industrial Building, which was right next to the powerhouse. (Both buildings are now gone; at the time of this story, only the powerhouse had been torn down.) The group was outside the Industrial Building, standing in the street chatting after their investigation. Their recorder, which they had left running, caught a spirit voice saying, *"I'm cold."*

Christina was puzzled by this. The powerhouse was the source of the steam heat that warmed every building on the hilltop. Was it a dangerous place? You betcha. Several workers met their ends in scalding accidents working around the blistering steam.

But why on earth would someone complain of being cold?

The answer lay in the Biennial Report for 1910. A patient was going about his business at the powerhouse, blissfully unaware of the tragedy that was about to snuff out his life. Heavy snow had fallen in central Illinois in the preceding days, and the roof of the building was piled high with snow. The sweltering heat inside had melted the bottom layer of snow, nearest the roof, over the previous few days. The melted snow had then refrozen into a thick layer of ice. The next day, the cycle had begun again.

Now, days later, there was an ice dam forming on top of the powerhouse roof. A layer of freezing cold water, a layer of ice, and a thick layer of snow had collected on the roof. The weight and stress were just too much. On March 5, 1910, the roof collapsed under the weight of several tons of ice and snow, and the ice dam slid into the jagged hole, sending an avalanche thundering down into the building, and crushing the work-man who happened to be standing in the wrong place at the wrong time. The patient probably never knew what hit him.

He only knew, *"I'm cold"*.

More detective work has led to an interesting theory about one of the more unnerving ghosts at the Pollak Hospital. In *Fractured Spirits*, I wrote about a spirit that wanders the hallways and the Men's Ward, a spirit that Pollak staff have nicknamed Heavy Boots.

Heavy Boots seems to enjoy intimidating people—even scaring them. Fear is energy, strong energy, and spirits feed on that. Heavy Boots' signature move is to stomp up to people in the darkness, hoping to scare the paste out of them. Mediums, especially women, have sensed the presence of an aggressive male spirit in the Men's Death Ward. Heavy Boots is one of the very few ghosts on the hilltop that seems to go out of his way to scare people. An encounter with Heavy Boots is usually a late-night experience.

It was this last observation that got the historians thinking. The Peoria State Hospital was, obviously, a working hospital, which meant that it was functioning twenty-four hours a day, seven days a week. Patients had round-the-clock care—including third shift.

An article appeared in the local newspaper on October 12, with the ominous headline, "Beating Is Fatal to Illinois TB Patient." The article below told an incredible story ... incredible, but true.

James Spahr and Jesse Bonham were rooming at the Pollak in the 1950s. They had both been committed to the asylum about three years before. They had both picked up mild cases of tuberculosis, and were recovering in the Men's Ward.

One night, James came barreling up behind Jesse and (for reasons known only to himself) thwacked him right across the back with a broom handle. Jesse was, understandably, annoyed by this unprovoked attack.

So he picked up a floor polisher and beat the living crap out of James with it.

The retaliatory weapon was unwieldy, probably much more awkward to lift and heft than a simple broom handle, but it did the trick. James died at the scene from the injuries Jesse inflicted on him. With a *floor polisher*. Jesse, after being examined by psychiatrists, was later removed to a "secure" hospital. (Which most likely meant a stretch in a hospital for the criminally insane.)

So here we have an attack in the wee hours of the night, an attack that ends in a violent beating death. These were both young men, full of piss and vinegar: Jesse was only 25, and James, the victim, was 33. The spirit that was left behind after this tragedy might be carrying an immense load of both guilt and anger—the perfect recipe for making a ghost. James probably had, in his mind, a perfectly good reason to whap Jesse with the broom handle. He probably also had zero clue that Jesse would overreact the way he did.

Heavy Boots, with his aggressive footsteps that give him a loud, sometimes menacing approach, is quite possibly the spirit of James. Let's face it—getting pulped by a floor polisher would leave someone with a *lot* of unresolved issues. Remember, death doesn't seem to change people's basic nature. This spirit, who was belligerent during his life, seems to have carried that attitude with him across to the Other Side.

In past years, Pollak investigations have included historical scenes in the initial walkthrough of the building. Actors in costume recreated events in the asylum's history, to bring the stories to life for the investigators.

One of the scenes was the story of the dietician who was killed in the 1960s. At that time, there was a patient at the asylum named James Sample. He had grown up in Minonk, Illinois, and he was an ethereally handsome young man—"angelically beautiful", some people said.

He was also batshit crazy. A childhood friend—if indeed Sample *had* any friends—remembered standing with Sample on a platform on some scaffolding at the very top of a water tower. The two boys were taking a break from their painting chore, looking out over the countryside from their perch when Sample turned to the other kid and mused, "You know, I could push you off this tower, and no one would ever know what happened."

Sample made several more comments like this around town, and people in the small town grew ... concerned. The general consensus in Minonk was that Sample was completely unstable, and should be locked away in some safe place. That safe place turned out to be the Peoria State Hospital. By the time he got to the asylum, his mania had progressed. He may have had the face of a Renaissance angel, but James actually had a full-blown, straight-up God complex. (His diagnosis was "mania with religious overtones".) He insisted on carrying "the Staff of God" around with him everywhere he went. And who would carry such a thing? Why, God himself.

Sometimes this Staff was a crowbar, sometimes it was simply a stick. (Sample really honestly was unhinged.) The attendants at the asylum quickly grew used to Sample's mania, and would sometimes gently take the Staff from him. "Hey, James, let's leave the stick outside for the night, huh? It's time for bed now." Gentle approaches like that seemed to calm him, and for a while, all was peaceful in Sample's world.

At the time, milk deliveries came in big metal cans. To open the cans, you'd break the seal and pry the metal lid free. Sample worked in the kitchen at the asylum, and would have been expected to open these cans. On this particular day, the Staff of God was a small crowbar. Sample chose to carry it with him constantly, even while he worked. When he was allowed to have the Staff with him, he worked diligently, without giving any of the attendants any trouble.

He was working in the kitchen on D Ward, with that day's Staff of God tucked underneath his arm, when his stilted, inefficient movements caught the attention of the new dietician. She had been on the job for just a couple of days, and according to the stories, she was very brusque with the patients, and didn't know how to relate to them very well. She watched Sample work awkwardly for a few moments, as she got more and more irritated with him. Finally she marched over to him, tugged the metal bar from under the crook of his elbow, set it down on the counter, and snapped, "Use both hands."

Well! This was the Staff of God she had just defiled. And you do *not* touch the Staff without God's permission. James Sample grabbed the Staff and smote the unbeliever with it. The force of the blow split her skull; she was probably dead before she hit the floor. Several attendants, nurses, and even patients piled onto Sample and brought him down. A couple of nurses were injured in the fracas, but the dietician was the only casualty. "God" did show his own kind of mercy; James only killed the dietician and severely injured nurses and other staff. He didn't hurt his fellow patients. But James Sample had used up his chances at the asylum. He went to prison after the attack.

This is one of the most well-known stories of the asylum, and it does hold resonance for many people because it did happen relatively recently. So the folks in charge of the historical scenes decided to use this incident. Part of the Women's Ward was turned into the "kitchen", with a counter set up, and behind it, shelves and appliances formed the suggestion of an institution kitchen. Utensils, pots and pans, and baking sheets rounded out the stage dressing.

I enjoy helping out with Pollak tours as much as I can, so that spring and summer, I volunteered to be part of one of the historical recreations. I got to play the ill-fated dietician. Brian, a long-time Pollak volunteer, acted as the Narrator, who told audiences the story. And a good-looking high school kid named Evan played James Sample.

We were the last scene on the tour, simply because of geographical fact—the slide show that begins every tour was presented in the Men's Death Ward, and the Women's Ward is on the opposite end of the building. Our scene was fairly short. The Narrator stood by and told the story in a nutshell, as "James" and I worked in the kitchen. "James" set biscuits on a baking sheet, working with a crowbar tucked underneath his arm, as I watched, fuming with increasing frustration. Then I stomped over, roughly snatched the crowbar from him, slammed it on the counter, and ordered, "Use both hands!" Then I walked away as "James" came to a slow boil. Ignoring him, I walked through a door at the far end of the kitchen and let it slam behind me.

Now, behind this door (spoilers!) was a seat cushion from

a car. Evan would follow me through the door, and raise the crowbar as the door closed, hiding us both from the audience. I would let out a brief scream, and Evan would smack the bejesus out of the seat cushion with the crowbar. He'd whale away for several blows, with the crowbar making very satisfying thwacks on the vinyl. Then he'd come back out through the door, breathing heavily and acting agitated. Brian would rush to calm him down, patting his shoulders, then turn to the audience of ghost hunters, saying, "You'd better leave. Come on, let's go." And he would lead them back through the building to the Men's Ward. The evening's investigation proper would start soon after that.

On one of these tours, James Barrow, an investigator with Spirits in the Night, was a guest. James likes to have a recorder running constantly, and he's wise to do so. You never know when you're going to catch a stray EVP.

The group crowded into the Women's Ward for the last scene of the walkthrough. As the Narrator spoke, and we went through the scene, Barrow caught a couple of comments by invisible audience members. As the Narrator said, "The one thing James Sample had to have with him at all times was the Staff of God," a young girl's voice piped up, *"That's right!"* Completely oblivious to this, we continued the scene. I snatched the Staff of God from "James", slammed it down on the counter, and stormed out of the kitchen, and the swinging door closed behind me. "James" fumed for a few moments, then grabbed the crowbar and followed me out. He came through the door, I screamed, he thwacked the cushion a few times—and a male voice snapped, *"Bastard! James Sample was no angel."*

Of course, this incident didn't happen in the Pollak. It happened in the E-shaped building that still stands just across the street from the Pollak. D Ward was a hospital ward—not an actual named hospital, but a ward where sickly patients were housed and cared for. (As opposed to healthy patients, who lived in the cottages.) The two outside arms of the E were the Men's and Women's wings, and the middle of the E was where the patients came together for meals. It was in this part of the building that James was working in the kitchen. He wasn't ill, so he wasn't being treated there; that was where he was assigned to work.

The former D Ward is now home to several businesses. Workmen are in and out of the building at all hours, so some of them have run into spirit activity. The dietician's death was so sudden and so violent that yes, she has ended up as a ghost in the building. And she has retained the personality she had in life— rather uptight, insisting on things being done properly ... what my grandmother would have called "persnickety". According to those who have encountered her, she cannot fathom what she did to get herself beaten to death with a pry bar. She still thinks she was in the right to insist to James that he do his job properly.

Another very sad death (that has also resulted in a haunting) happened on the hilltop in the 1930s. A young woman who lived in one of the A Row cottages suffered from depression. (Some say there was a man involved, and that the woman's depression stemmed from unrequited love.) One day, she decided that she could no longer face the anguish she believed her life had become, so she ended it. She tied one end of a rope to a post of her bedstead, tied the other end around her neck, and slipped off the side of her bed to the floor. She died, not of hanging, but of strangulation—a very slow way to go.

People who have encountered her say that in the afterlife, she presents herself in much the same way as she lived. She appears as a phantom, but never makes a sound. She wants to be seen, but she doesn't feel as though she has anything to say.

The young lady's cottage was demolished years ago, but another building was put up in its place. Superior Autobody now sits at the location once occupied by that cottage. A grove of trees, planted decades ago when the asylum was thriving, their trunks forming a neat circle, still stands silent guard next to the building.

And this young lady still walks the grounds. People have seen her wandering through this grove of trees. She's been seen with her hands to her throat, as though she's choking.

D Ward, where James Sample bludgeoned the dietician with the Staff of God. The attack took place in the middle leg of the building.

INSANE PATIENT SUICIDES

PEORIA, ILL.—Mrs. Anna Port-
sheller, 35, an inmate of the Peoria
state hospital for the insane, used
the belt of her dress in committing
suicide by hanging yesterday, fas-
tening it to the headboard of her
bed and then rolling out of bed.
She was committed to the hospital
from Washington, Ill.

DYNAMITE

Was Used By the Aged Madman To
Blow His Head From
His Body.

SPECIAL DISPATCH TO THE ENQUIRER.

Peoria, Ill., August 15.—Charles P. Jones,
aged 73, whose home is at Hanna City,
Ill., blew his head off with a dynamite
cartridge in a ravine near the Peoria State
Hospital for the Insane to-day.

Jones was admitted to the asylum August
3 on his own request. His case was but a
mild one and he chatted cheerfully with the
nurses a few nights before he committed
his rash act. He had the freedom of the
grounds and doubtless got the dynamite
cartridge from a near-by coal mine.

The blast severed his head from the body
as if done by a guillotine, and while nothing could be found of the head, the body
was in good shape.

Beating Is Fatal To Illinois TB Patient

PEORIA, Ill., Oct. 12. (INS)—A 33-year-old tubercular patient at Peoria state hospital was beaten to death today by a fellow patient wielding a floor polisher.

The victim, James Spahr, of Canton, Ill., had been sharing a room in the tubercular section with his slayer, Jesse Bonham, 25, of Pekin, Ill. Both had been mental patients.

Assistant hospital superintendent H. B. Knowles quoted Bonham as saying Spahr attacked him suddenly.

Dr. Knowles said both men were admitted to the hospital about three years ago as separate mental cases. He said they were transferred to the tubercular section when they developed mild cases of the disease.

Peoria County Coroner Chauncey Wood said an inquest into Spahr's death would be held tomorrow. Wood said he would recommend that Bonham be examined by state alienists and transferred to a "secure" hospital.

conditioned, for $2,010.00 each.

Woman Hospital Worker Killed

BARTONVILLE, Ill. (AP) — A woman employe of the Peoria State Hospital was bludgeoned to death Monday by a male patient who also battered three other women with a piece of pipe.

Mrs. Julianna S. McDonald, 62, a dietician, died shortly after the attack. Mrs. Wanda Johnson, 47, supervisor of the building where the attacks occurred, was severely beaten. Her condition was critical.

LOST BUILDINGS

From 1902 to 1973, when the Peoria State Hospital was open for business, the landscape of the hilltop was constantly shifting. The asylum expanded, new buildings were put up, hospitals and cottages were added to serve the needs of the patients. Even before the asylum opened, buildings were going up—and coming down.

The Peoria Women's Club pushed for the asylum as early as 1889, principally to get people with mental illness out of the almshouses of the state and into state care. Dr. Zeller was appointed as the superintendent in July 1898, a bit prematurely, as it turned out. In July 1898, there was no staff, there were no patients, and there was no salary. So Dr. Zeller volunteered as a surgeon for the army, and went off to the Philippines to serve in the Spanish-American War.

The Kirkbride plan was a very popular design for mental hospitals in the nineteenth century. Designed by Thomas Kirkbride, an architect who was also an expert on the mentally ill, the Kirkbride building was a massive structure meant to house all of the patients at an asylum. These buildings were arranged with a central part where the superintendent and his wife would live, and a wing off to each side, a men's wing and a women's wing. As the patient population grew, workers could add onto the end of each wing, expanding outward as needed. The Kirkbride was actually a pretty good design. The wings were fairly narrow, with rooms on each side of the hallway. This meant, in theory, that patients could look out onto the grounds of the asylum and have a pleasant view no matter where their rooms were located.

In practice, though, the design had some serious drawbacks. There was no arrangement made to separate patients according to the severity of their illness. So a patient with a mild case of, say, epilepsy could have a raving schizophrenic as their roommate. This doesn't do either one of them any good. Kirkbride buildings all over the country were also prone to overcrowding, cramming more and more patients in, to the detriment of their care.

And the Kirkbride building in Bartonville was, to put it bluntly, a hot mess. The builders were none too choosy about their building materials. So by the time the building was finished, it was already settling, and cracks were developing in the foundation. The ventilation shafts didn't link together, and the walls weren't even plumb, that's how shoddy the construction was on this building.

Dr. Zeller toured the Kirkbride before he left for the Philippines. He was one of several men in the running for the position of superintendent. He noted the poor ventilation, the cracks in the foundation, the general jankiness of the whole thing. He declared the building unfit for anyone, let alone mental patients. He was never a fan of the Kirkbride plan for asylums anyway. After inspection, the state of Illinois said tear it down and start over. And that's exactly what happened. Part of the basement of the original building became the east part of the Levitin Hospital. And the limestone blocks of the foundation were re-used as the foundation for several other buildings, including the Mitchell Hospital, the first hospital of the asylum.

In the meantime, Dr. Zeller was appointed superintendent. He'd been considering another stint in the Army, but the Women's Club offered him the position because they wanted him in Illinois, not halfway around the world helping with the Spanish-American War.

For his part, Dr. Zeller was pleasantly relieved that the public department of welfare decided to go with a cottage system, rather than putting up another Kirkbride building. In the cottage system, first developed at the Illinois Eastern Hospital for the Insane in Kankakee in September 1879, patients with similar ailments were housed together—epileptics with epileptics, alcoholics with alcoholics, and so on. This provided the patients with a web of support and understanding from their peers, the people they lived with every day. It turned out to be a much more effective way of treating the mentally ill.

Dr. Zeller took charge of his asylum in November 1902. He was very hands-on when it came to running the hilltop. It was his decision to put up solariums with colored glass windows to treat patients. He was a big proponent of color therapy, which is the theory that color can affect our health and attitude. For example, red increases respiration rate, green acts as a relaxant and fights depression, and blue calms breathing and heart rate. This is a theory that is still very much in use today.

Tuberculosis was a scourge on the hilltop from the very beginning of the hospital's history. In fact, 90 % of the patients that passed away on the hilltop died from tuberculosis. Dr. Zeller knew that patients showing signs of the disease had to be isolated, to keep the insidious illness from spreading through the entire patient population. Dr. Zeller had Dining Hall A pressed into service as a tuberculosis ward for female patients. This included putting canvas tents on the west and south sides of the building, to give patients fresh air. These tents were put up because Dining Hall A didn't have porches built onto it. Patients had to enjoy these westerly and southerly breezes in the tents.

Even when the hospitals opened, the Levitin for female patients and the batwing hospital for those suffering from tuberculosis, these buildings were still used as hospital wards. Dining Hall A didn't see an easing of patients until 1929, during another flush of construction.

And that is why, even today, the yard of Dining Hall A is one of the hot spots for paranormal phenomena on the hilltop. The tents are long gone, but female spirits are still seen gathered on the west and south sides of the building where the sheltering tents used to be. If you stand very still at the curb facing the building, and listen, you might hear quiet wisps of girlish conversation carried to you on the breeze.

The hospital's willingness to use a dining hall as patient housing speaks volumes to the ingenuity and flexibility of the institution. One of these brilliant and practical ideas was the use of canvas houses. These were two-story houses made of wood with canvas stretched tightly over them to form walls. These buildings, portable and completely temporary, were used whenever there was an outbreak of disease on the hilltop—and there were several. Pellagra, influenza, and yellow fever were just a few of the illnesses that ravaged the institution from time to time. (Pellagra was a vitamin deficiency that could have horrific results. The yellow fever outbreaks were simply a result of the asylum's proximity to the Illinois River, which was much marshier in the first half of the twentieth century than it is now—and the riverbank can still get pretty gooey at certain times of the year. The mosquitoes are still vicious in the summer. And the influenza epidemic of 1918 did not spare the hilltop.)

These temporary buildings were expressly designed to keep patients in quarantine until the threat of the outbreak had passed. Instead of devoting an entire building to housing victims of an outbreak, the staff could keep just the affected patients out of the general population until they knew how serious the situation was. Of course, diseases came and went, and came again, in the era before antibiotics. So these canvas houses would pop up like mushrooms on the hilltop. They were used as needed, then dismantled until the next crisis came along.

If the problem was serious enough, like tuberculosis, the asylum would put up a permanent building to house the patients. For this reason, sometimes the hauntings are older than the building, because they started even before the hospital was built.

These canvas houses have gone for decades. Absolutely no trace of them remains. So what does this mean for the paranormal investigator who wanders the asylum grounds? It means that anywhere you go on the hilltop, you could be standing where one of these houses was put up ... and where perhaps dozens of patients died before an epidemic ran its course. These were, in effect, portable death houses. If you go exploring anywhere on the grounds, on any flat place, next to any of the ravines, there's a very good chance that you are standing side by side with someone who remains here.

Think about that the next time you wander outside Club 309 for a cigarette.

"ASYLUM GIRL"

Kids can be jerks.

High school isn't necessarily "the best years of your life"—not for those of us who are out of step with the expected pace of modern teen life. Christina Morris discovered, as did many of us, that those four years ain't all a John Hughes movie.

"Back in the day, in the 1980s and stuff, you didn't run around with cameras like people do today. So it wasn't until Publications class that it really dawned on me that I should bring a camera up here, to the asylum grounds. I wanted to do stories about the old asylum."

Christina had been fascinated by the Peoria State Hospital since she'd been a little girl of seven. Her grandfather would bring her up to the hilltop to visit a relative who is buried in one of the cemeteries. When her grandfather gently explained that the Peoria State Hospital was a place for "special people", young Christina gazed at the imposing stone bulk of the Bowen Building and immediately guessed what made these people special: they were giants.

As Christina grew out of childhood, she understood that it wasn't giants who lived on the hilltop. But her respect for the asylum's residents never faded—in fact, it grew as she learned more about the institution.

"When I presented my ideas to the Publications teacher, she had it in her head that it was a torture institution, and she didn't really want to do stories about an old, closed institution. She'd rather I wrote stories about Madonna and things like that."

But Christina didn't give up. She was determined to tell the true story of the Peoria State Hospital. And her Publications class was the perfect outlet for this. Or so she thought.

"Back in high school, there were quite a few guys who would play the 'Mine' game. The game was based on a points system. If you were near someone who, say, fell down the stairs, if you hollered out 'Mine!' and pointed at them, it was worth so many points to you. So if someone fell down the stairs in an avalanche of books and papers and feet, some teenage boy would yell 'Mine!', and that's three points to the person who yelled it out and brought more attention to somebody's embarrassing moment.

"If they provided the embarrassing moment, it was higher in points. The dumber or weirder it was, it was higher in points. So if they came up behind you and they pushed your face into the water fountain while you were getting a drink, that was five or six points. They'd yell 'Mine', and it was funny, because you got water on your face. It wasn't really bullying, because you're not getting hit, you're not getting hurt, you got water on your face.

"They especially liked it when you said something they thought was stupid or weird. Well, we were in Publications class, and this was the second time I'd suggested a story about the asylum. I think this time I even tried to drum up some interest by mentioning ghosts, because I was desperate for her to let me write *something* about the asylum.

"At this point, one of the boys looks at me and goes, 'What asylum?' I started to say, 'There's an old asylum on the hilltop in Bartonville, it's got a lot of old history to it …' Right as I'm starting to talk about it, he stands up in the middle of class, points at my face, and screams 'MIIINE! That's gotta be a good nine points! We got the asylum girl here!' To them it was hysterical that I was this interested. I just thought it was cool."

From then on, Christina Morris was known around campus as Asylum Girl. The clique of boys who played the Mine game took great delight in yelling out how many points the first kid had gotten from her.

"Yelling 'Asylum Girl' at me like they did, I think they thought it was hurting me, but it wasn't. It did let me know, throughout my life, it taught me to keep that kind of stuff close to the vest."

Christina has been fighting the stigma of the abandoned mental asylum for most of her life. It's the love she has for the place that keeps her going, that helps her to ignore the haters, that feeds her desire to share the true history of the Peoria State Hospital with the world.

She paints a beautiful picture of the asylum grounds as they looked soon after the institution closed, before the area was turned into an industrial park. "People these days don't get to see the hilltop the way I saw it when I was exploring it. Between the buildings, there was just open ground, and the wildflowers had taken off. This whole hilltop was just covered with wild-flowers between the cottages. And the zoo had fallen apart, so the ravines used to be just thick with the deer and the turkeys that had gotten out of the zoo."

Christina's gray eyes dance with the memory. "You'd come up the hill from the river and you'd crest the top of the hill where the Zeller Hospital was, and there would be thousands of deer. It was amazing—you'd be coming up out of the tunnel system, and it would sound like a damn stampede up here, because there'd be so many deer going from one ravine to the other. It was beautiful.

"I couldn't stop coming up here. I couldn't stop reading about it. And every time I came up here, there was more to find. I had pieces of uniforms, pieces of shoes. I had sheets with the Peoria State Hospital logo on them, that came from the Bowen. Some of it got thrown away, you know, like your grandma coming across your baseball cards in the attic and getting rid of them because she doesn't know what they are. My ex-husband threw some of it away, and if I had that now … boxes of reports, dietary files, nurses' papers, all kinds of stuff that would really let you into the life of this hospital. As people started to tear it up, I wanted to save it. I wanted to show it to people and not lose it. That's what gave me the idea to start a museum.

"People said, you're crazy. Nobody cares about this history enough to want to visit a museum about some crazy lunatic asylum." Now, sitting in the neat main room of a museum that sees at least a thousand visitors a year, Christina can smile at the idea. The museum is the first stop on any paranormal tour of the Pollak. It's open during the huge Old Hospital Bazaar every year. And sometimes, people will wander in just out of curiosity. Christina welcomes them all.

"I let people know on a regular basis that not only will we continue to provide history on the hilltop, we'll continue to correct it. When you find new information, you have to add it to the storyline you already have. I have no problem saying, hey, this is the only information we had at the time but guess what we found! That's gonna happen in an institution that ran for seventy-one years and had thousands of people living in it."

The Peoria State Hospital Museum has another mission, too. In addition to providing displays of artifacts and access to hundreds of newspaper articles, Christina also gives talks to nursing students, thus keeping alive the Peoria State Hospital tradition of teaching. She gives two tours a year to nursing students, for two different psychiatric training programs. To the younger students at Illinois Central College, the ones who are just starting their training, Christina gives full-on history lectures. The older students, the ones from OSF Hospital, are the graduating class, who have already started to work on the wards. These students get treated to a talk on some of the different therapies used at the Peoria State Hospital. Some of these, like cold wrap therapy, are coming back into practice in modern times. The students are stunned that these old practices are becoming accepted again. This is something they may have used on a patient just last week, and here it was being done at the asylum in the 1920s.

Now let's take a look at the paranormal side of things. Christina's passion for history spills over into the paranormal aspects of the hilltop. The history and the ghost stories are so intertwined that it's hard to separate them sometimes. Christina is glad that people are starting to discover the asylum, no matter which angle they approach it from.

"This hilltop is a battery of charge. You just feel it, and it's so welcoming. I know a lot of paranormally active places have more of a scary feeling. When you're here on this hilltop, you feel the energy and you feel the paranormal and you feel the hair stand up on the back of your neck and you get the goose-bumps—but it's because you know that they *want* you to see them. They *want* to interact with you. The same way that you're getting this charge, they're getting that charge off of you. I think this is the exact reason why there are hundreds and hundreds of EVPs that have been caught on these grounds. There have been hundreds of videos, lots of ghost footage captured, in the buildings and in all the surrounding areas, all the time, because of that constant battery charge of people coming here.

"I also think that it's pretty self-evident that it's not an evil energy. With all of the kids who came up here in the 1980s, I never knew a kid to get hurt in any other way than other kids messing around. Their terrifying experiences happened because somebody did something like that to them, left them behind, locked them in a room, those kind of things. It was kids trying to be funny in the dark, playing pranks on their friends."

Along with her passion for history, Christina is also highly aware of the supernatural aspect of the asylum. So why is she now willing to open up about her paranormal experiences? Christina has been studying the asylum and its history for thirty years. She's been leading tours and promoting history in a professional capacity for twelve years. She has run countless tours, both historical and paranormal. She has organized the Old State Hospital Bazaar, that brings vendors from the community together on the hilltop. She has put together the Peoria State Hospital Museum. She has proven, to herself and to anyone who asks, that she is saving the historical aspect of the institution. She has spent years of her life fighting for legitimacy, for recognition.

And now? Well, the simple truth is that times have changed. The world at large is more open these days to claims of paranormal experiences. Someone who has had a brush with the paranormal no longer has to be afraid of being seen as unprofessional if they share it with the world. Having a connection to the supernatural no longer makes someone an oddball.

She knows that the Peoria State Hospital is a magnet for ghost hunters, and she encourages that. The more people that come for the ghost hunting, the bigger an audience Christina has to share the incredible history of the asylum with. In order to give paranormal investigators the best experience they can get, Christina has put a lot of thought into the paranormal side of the coin.

"You go to a paranormal site where one bad thing happened, and there may be a ghost or two. This is a hilltop filled with people who had bad things happen to them throughout most of their lives! This was their one place to find refuge, their haven from the world outside, which could be terrifying.

"You have to keep in mind the fact that spirits see themselves in the afterlife the way they saw themselves in life. Most paranormalists know this, because they'll see a woman or have ghost footage of a woman who looks young, and they find out that she died in her seventies. Well, she's going to see herself in the prime of her life, and that's usually in your youth."

(Our own Rhoda Derry is the perfect example of this. She died the day before she would have turned seventy-two, yet she appears as a vibrant young woman—the way she probably would have looked if she had married Charles Phenix.)

"It's the same way with mental patients. If they thought of themselves as invisible, we may now see them as a puff of smoke. If they saw themselves as a black mass, if they were depressed, we might now see them as that black growing shadowy mass that comes down the hallway. If they saw themselves as a young healthy person, before the tuberculosis ravaged them, they're going to present themselves as that young healthy person, because they want you to see them the way they saw themselves."

Christina loves the hilltop, but she's under no delusions that life here was roses and unicorns all the time. "Is every EVP up here going to be how they loved it? No. Do we have those? Yes. But we also have EVPs that say things that are completely off the wall, because the *patients* said and did things that were completely off the wall. Some of them were violent, and their ghosts will come up on you and give you a fright, because they were violent in life. Some of the patients were loving and childlike. You could be hearing an EVP that sounds like a child, and really, you're talking to a fifty year old man. It's almost like being catfished by the spirits, because they're going to present themselves the way they saw and felt themselves in life."

She is also very pragmatic about her ghost tours, and what people can expect from them. "Ghosts are not freakin' popcorn. I can't put a bag in the microwave and serve them up to you. We're not Disneyland. We're not going to fake stuff for you. But we've found that the more honest, the more forthright, the more laid-back we are, and the more information we have, the better the paranormal investigation will be."

Christina has some very good advice for paranormal investigators that are just starting out in the field. "I've seen a lot of paranormalists who can't wait to have their first experience, and yet, the first thing they do is hightail it out of there. I think that happens more often than anything when someone finally gets their first experience. So I would stress to anyone who's investigating on this hilltop: *Stay*. Hold on. Wait. Experience. Nothing here is going to hurt you. With all the years I've been here and all the tours I've led, and the thousands of people that have walked this hilltop with me, no one's ever been damaged in any way. If that weren't true, I'd never lead another tour on the hilltop.

"The reason I lead tours on this hilltop is because I truthfully, honestly and from the bottom of my heart can tell you, without a shadow of a doubt, that the spirits here enjoy the tours just as much as the people who come to visit them."

DR. GEORGE ZELLER

Back in the 1980s, when ghost stories really started to gain traction in Bartonville, one apparition seemed to appear with regularity. Witnesses would describe a tall, lanky man, who was sometimes seen wearing a top hat. This particular image would always be seen at a distance. Christina Morris has a theory about the specter.

"It's Dr. Zeller. And why would he choose to keep his distance? Because he still considers himself the superintendent of this institution. His job is not to interact one-on-one with you, his job is to watch over his entire institution. Dr. Zeller is still interested in what's happening on this hilltop.

"I think that's responsible for the sadness some people feel who witness his ghost—this is not what he intended. But when you get close to what he intended, then you feel that it's right, that you have his approval. I think people feel that up here, and I don't necessarily mean that paranormally. Even small businesses up here, once their business is up and going, we'll hear some of them say that they've had the image of a man appear, and they've felt the warmth of success. This was a man who was all about success. I think he is happy with the fact that the hilltop is still alive and thriving."

Dr. Zeller still has a presence on the hilltop. But it's quite possible that he keeps himself removed from daily life, because he himself didn't believe in the paranormal. He doesn't see himself as being beyond the Veil. He still sees himself as being in charge.

There is a fun exception to this habit of distance Dr. Zeller has. Many times, George will hang out in a doorway, watching whatever is going on inside a room with tolerant amusement. He seems to enjoy looking in on a work party of volunteers as they paint sets for the haunt or clean up one of the Pollak rooms. Work parties, especially those where the teens get involved, can get pretty rowdy. They're having fun being together, playing music, and doing something good for the memory of the asylum. George will look on bemusedly, almost as if he wants to step into the room to supervise the volunteers. It's as if he wants to say, "Okay, yes, I know you're having fun, but don't forget to get something accomplished too."

TOUR OF THE HILLTOP

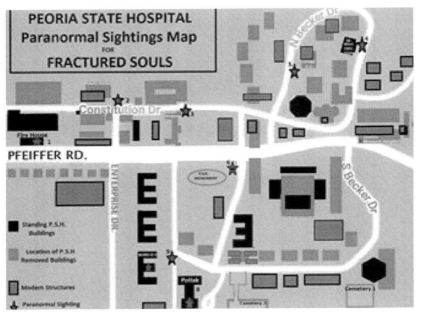

By now, I've told you story after story about the Peoria State Hospital. You know that some of the asylum buildings are still around, while some have fallen to the wrecking ball. Even though the look of the area has changed significantly since 1973, you can still experience the hilltop for yourself.

With help from Christina Morris, I've put together a self-guided tour of the asylum grounds. You can experience this from your car, or you can park and walk the circuit. Keep in mind that when the asylum grounds were laid out in 1898, they were actually designed with foot traffic in mind.

As you walk or drive this loop, I'll point out places important to the asylum's history. I'll let you know, if you're driving,
where you can get out of your car and walk around. We'll also
let you know if a landmark is now private property. (If it is, I
ask that you respect this, and just look from your car or from
the curb. Please don't trespass; it's not cool.) But do remember
the "curb to curb" rule. If you are standing on the curb, or in
the street, that's public property, and you have every right in
the world to be there. You can videotape, you can take photos,
anything you like. Heck, Google Earth does it all day long.

Also, here's something cool: if you have a smart phone, feel
free to turn to the back pages of the book. There, you'll find
a couple of QR codes for you to scan. One will take you to a
special episode of Lights Out, my podcast of true ghost stories.
This will be an audio version of this guided tour. The other code
will take you to a website where you can watch costumed actors
recreate scenes from the asylum's history. And now you'll know
where these things happened.

Don't be shy about just pulling off to the side of the road.
Roll down your windows, be quiet, and see what happens. If a
cop rolls up and asks you what you're doing, go ahead and tell
them. The police up here know exactly why people come to the
hilltop. (Especially if you're sitting in your car. That lets you be
up here at night without being *too* obvious.)

If you do decide to get out of your car if you're driving,
or do this as a walking tour, I highly encourage you to bring
some ghost hunting tools with you. (If that's why you're here,
of course. If you're just here for the history, that's cool too. Just
disregard this next part.) Don't worry if you're taking this tour
on a bright sunny day. Not all ghost experiences happen on
dark stormy nights, at midnight, or at three in the morning. You
can have a perfectly legitimate paranormal experience in the
middle of the afternoon. If you're standing there, alone, talking
into the woods, and you get somebody talking back? That's an
EVP—I don't care if it happens at nine o'clock at night or nine
o'clock in the morning.

So bring a camera with you. Bring a KII meter. Bring a voice
recorder. When you pause at these sites, especially at the hot

spots I'm going to tell you about, go ahead and take some pictures. Ask some questions, if you're so inclined. Listen to that recording later. Someone may have responded to your questions.

Or just stand still and soak in the atmosphere around you. Open yourself to the sounds of Bartonville.

You may discover that you're not alone.

Let's start at the Firehouse. It's a perfectly appropriate place to begin our tour, as it's the oldest building on the hilltop. It's the brown brick building with the big plate glass window. There's a sign on the window that says Peoria State Hospital Museum. Park your car there, if you're walking, and let's go for a stroll.

Before you leave the parking lot, though, stand with your back to the firehouse and look towards the water tower. To the left of the water tower, down where those orange and white construction barrels are sitting, that's where the train tracks were, that served the hilltop. The powerhouse was on the north side of the tracks, and deliveries of coal were dropped off there. The general storehouse was on the other side of the tracks, closer to us (on the south side of the south track). Patients were dropped off from the south track, and so were supplies. Supplies were either taken right into the general storehouse or taken from the train platform to wherever they were needed on the hilltop.

The Powerhouse
The powerhouse is no longer standing. This is the building whose roof collapsed on the unfortunate worker.

Turn right (west) out of the museum parking lot. Turn right again (north) at the first stop sign you come to, which is Ricketts. Your first right after that will be Constitution Drive. This will put you heading east.

This is actually the front entrance of the asylum grounds. Pfeiffer Road, which nowadays cuts right through the middle of the grounds, was only used by the people who lived in that area and by people coming to work at the Employee's Building (Bowen Building).

About halfway down this long block, just a little past the water tower (which is now on your right), there's a light post on the left side of the street, near a low wall of concrete blocks. Let's stop here for a moment. Look behind you, back towards the water tower. Draw your gaze in closer, next to the street. See that ramp? That's all that's left of the storehouse.

Now, across the street, this is where the Powerhouse and the Industrial Building once stood. Stand at the light post and look back towards that gray building. Where it dips down in front of the driveway, that's where the boiler system was. Where the light is, on the front door of the building, would have been about the middle of the powerhouse. And under this streetlight was where Christina Morris and her friends captured the *"I'm cold"* EVP described in the chapter on "Mysterious Deaths and Murders".

Go just a bit farther up the street. There, on the right—see where that crumbling retaining wall turns into a pristine new wall of concrete blocks? And do you see the grassy field beyond the retaining wall, that stretches off to your right? That's where the Bowen Building used to be.

Continuing on, we'll cross Becker Drive. The water treatment plant is on your left, on the northeast corner of the intersection. This is the Octagon Building, which used to be the combined commissary, barber shop, and beauty shop. It also functioned as a maintenance building, a domestic building, and a dining hall throughout its life. Follow this road as it curves around to the left, and very soon, Dining Hall A will be on your left. The road makes a loop—let's stop before the road curves left again.

On your right, to the east, there is a ravine. Dining Hall A was actually tapped for use as a tuberculosis ward due to its situation at this site, which was on purpose. Cool breezes drift up from that well-shaded gully. The hilltop is criss-crossed with ravines, and in the days before central air conditioning, buildings were constructed with these breezes in mind.

Womens Infirmary. A former mess hall now admirably caring for sixty infirm women.

Dining Hall A.

See the lights way past the ravine, where those apartment buildings are? That's where the Kirkbride building used to stand, and later, the Talcott Hospital farther to the east. (They couldn't build directly on the former site of the Kirkbride because that's where all the construction problems had cropped up in the first place, with an unstable foundation. It was eventually just used as a parking lot.)

Farther even beyond that, you'll find the top of the hillside staircase. But don't go searching for it too assiduously. You have to cross private property to get to the stairs, and the staircase itself is the property of the city of Bartonville. And if you come up the stairs from the bottom of the hill, that's Keystone property. And either one of those organizations will call the law on you. Besides, the stairs are old and decrepit, and at this point, they're not very safe. So just … don't even bother with it.

But let's turn back to Dining Hall A, which is far more interesting anyway. It's on the inside of the loop. Dining Hall A is a quietly elegant building, brown brick with a darker brown roof. Every window has a tidy, graceful arch over it. The tents for the tuberculosis patients were set up off of the south and west sides of the building. So, if you're looking at the building from the road, that's the left side of the building, which is fenced off, and the far side, which you can't see from here. But! This entire yard was theirs, it was the tuberculosis yard. This entire place is filled with the ladies who once lived here.

A quick note of caution here: there are apartment buildings right across the street, so try not to make too much noise. (And hey, if you're ghost hunting, you're going to want to be quiet anyway.) I say this for two reasons. First off, people live there, so we don't want to intrude on their privacy. Second off, you'd be amazed at the whispers you might hear on the wind at Dining Hall A, if you give it a chance.

Dining Hall A with the tent colony set up on the sides.

Moving on, we'll follow the road as it curves around to the left again. There are still dark, deliciously creepy woods on your left, on the outside of the loop formed by the road. On the inside of the loop is where the A Row Cottages once stood.

Let's pause again, now that the road has straightened out. On our left is Superior Autobody. Next to it is a pretty little circular grove of evergreen trees, mostly firs, with a couple of white pines thrown in too. Get this—those trees have been there since the early days of the asylum. They were planted when the A Row cottages were built way back in 1902. When Dr. Zeller walked the hilltop, these thirty-foot tall trees were just tiny saplings, their bases wrapped in burlap. How cool is that?

What's even cooler is that the spirit of the young woman who committed suicide by strangulation in her room in one of the A Row cottages (as described in the chapter "Mysterious Deaths and Murders") has been seen in this grove of trees.

A Row Cottages. See the teensy saplings between the two cottages? They grew up into the majestic circle of trees you see today.

We're at the stop sign at North Becker Drive and Constitution Drive, but we're not going to go straight. We're going to turn right, then hang a quick left. (I brought you to this street, rather than going straight on Becker, because this road we're on is part of the original asylum campus road system. Becker is a modern cut-through.) We're heading south now on Industry, towards Pfeiffer Road. We'll cross the road here.

If you're walking, stop when you've gotten across the road and turn around to face the road. Look up the road to your left. That's where the Bowen used to be, and that's where the Bowen Lady in White used to walk. Now look down the road to your right. See that ravine, with the woods that loom up on either side of the road? That's where the *other* Lady in White is seen, right on the road.

Head south on Industry, just for a block, until you get to a T intersection. Right in front of you, that building that looks like an abandoned grade school, that's the Pollak Hospital. Turn left, and park in the parking lot just to the left of the drive with the horse gate across it.

Now, if you follow this street (South Becker Drive) as it curves around back to Pfeiffer Road, just as it curves to the left, Cemetery One will be on the right. You can't really see it from the road; you'll have to leave the street and go down that grassy little swale. If you stand on that gentle slope and put your right hand up, that will give you the layout of Cemetery One. Your thumb is the part of the cemetery set aside for veterans; you'll recognize it because there's a little American flag on every single grave. The rest of your hand is the rest of Cemetery One. And about six rows back, where those bunches of flowers and the little white porcelain cherubs are, that's Rhoda Derry's grave.

But we're not at Cemetery One. We're still in the parking lot next to the horse gate. See that yellow post, with the sidewalk running out from it, into those lovely spooky trees? That's the way into Cemetery Two. We're going to walk down that side-walk. The trees will open up into a secretive, shady grove. About halfway down, you're going to see a bigger, lighter gravestone that doesn't match the others, which are a dull tan concrete. That's the purported site of Bookbinder's grave—but that's not who we're here to see.

Go over to that gravestone—the Pollak will be behind you—and look out towards the back of the cemetery, towards the tree line. Halfway along there is where the TAPS full-spectrum camera caught the shadow figure walking, from the middle of the tree line, heading to the right. That may have been our friend Mr. Dynamite.

Let's turn around and head towards the Pollak. We'll pass between two big trees that mark the entrance to Cemetery Two. An interesting EVP was captured here: a man's voice saying "*I did ...I died.*"

We can go around the side of the Pollak, or the front circle drive, it doesn't matter. We're headed to the lightpost at the corner of the Pollak side yard, at the corner of South Becker Drive and Enterprise. Look across Enterprise. See that huge red E-shaped building just across the street? That's the hospital ward where James Sample killed the dietician with one blow from the Staff of God. The kitchen where James was working was in the middle leg of the E, back where it meets the long part of the building.

I'm going to leave you here. There's much more to the hilltop to explore. But! You'll get to see that in the next book. I've shown you the buildings—and the vanished buildings—that have paranormal activity associated with them, and told you the stories. We are still discovering stories, from history and from the other side of the veil. There are many more tales to come, I promise. Stay tuned!

I hope you've enjoyed this peek into the past. Before you leave, take one last look around you. Remember, this was home to so many people. This was a place of safety. This was where people came to find help, and solace, and compassionate care, and understanding, and acceptance, no matter what problems bedeviled them. This was *home*.

Oh, and one more thing. Take a look at your phone.

Back in the days of the asylum's operation, the hilltop had its own phone exchange (the first three numbers that identify where a phone call originates from). This meant that anyone calling from one building to another simply had to dial the last four numbers. So if you happen to get a call or even a text on your phone, and the caller ID only shows four digits, someone may be trying to call you ... from the asylum's past.

CONCLUSION

A nd so we come nearly to the end of another book of people's experiences at the Peoria State Hospital. Keep in mind that the stories I've just shared with you are just the tales of spirits who have chosen to interact with us. There could be dozens of shades wandering the hilltop simply minding their own business, or hiding from human contact because they're still mired in the torments of their own mind. We could be strolling the cemeteries, or driving up Pfeiffer Road, or sitting down in a booth at the Phoenix Club for a burger, or perusing the stacks at Alpha Park Library, and pass handfuls of ghosts without even knowing it.

Thank you for letting me share these stories with you—not only the ghost stories, but also the history behind them. I'm not the only paranormal investigator with an equally intense passion for history. And it makes sense, to me and to others. You can't fully understand the ghost tales of a place without knowing the history behind them, because it was those human experiences that *led* to the ghost lore. And we, the historians, are also the keepers of the ghost stories. Look at it this way, if it helps: why would you trust a lawyer if you knew they'd never won a case? Why would you trust a paranormal investigator if they can't back up their ghost stories with historical facts?

Of course, this can be a double-edged sword. Do the historians catch flak for what they do, working in a haunted mental asylum? You bet they do. Christina Morris, historian for the Peoria State Hospital Museum, tells of one woman that came up to her after a tour with a complaint.

"You just keep the ghosts here to make money off of them,

and that's not right. You should set them free."

"We tell the spirits they can stay for as long as they like," Christina insisted to me later. This point is made abundantly clear to every paranormal tour that investigates the Pollak Hospital. Ghost hunters are strictly forbidden to try to "cross spirits over". In fact, they are even discouraged from using regular flashlights in the basement of the building, in case the spirits mistake them for the "white light" of the Other Side, and hide. It's a well-known fact of the basement that using a regular flashlight will shut any activity down cold, and that's the reason that happens. The spirits really don't like the white light.

(It's suggested that investigators use flashlights with red or green filters instead. Plus, colored light won't mess up your night vision the way white light will.)

The reason for this strict rule is quite simple. This is the spirits' home. Sometimes, it was the only home in which they knew peace and safety and comfort. Why on earth would anyone be so heartless as to kick them out of it? Or tell them they have to leave it?

"It's their choice to stay. That's between them and their God," Christina says.

And, delightfully, many of the spirits *have* chosen to stay. They add their spooky influence to many places on the hilltop. The Peoria State Hospital is known far and wide as a home for haunts.

That notoriety spills over into other aspects of the former asylum that have only a passing connection to the paranormal, or to history. The Haunted Infirmary, organized by Doom Industries every year, has been in the Top Ten Haunts in Illinois for the past eight years, and it's been in the number one spot for the past three years. Thanks to the Haunted Infirmary, the Pollak Hospital is no longer considered an endangered building. Haunts save history ... the Haunted Infirmary proves that every October, to the sound of hundreds of screams every weekend.

And that's why the Peoria State Hospital Museum is such a wonderful place. It's just another way for us to demonstrate the importance of saving this hilltop for the years ahead. Come for the ghosts, stay for the history. In fact, there are plenty of people who visit the museum just for its historical value. Many people who live in the area have relatives who are buried in one of our four cemeteries. The staff at the museum have an astounding success rate at finding the graves of these folks—if your relative was buried on the hilltop after 1930, three times out of four, the museum volunteers will be able to find that person for you. That's a 75 % rate of success. Not too shabby.

We know that it's scientifically impossible to destroy energy. You can never annihilate energy; you can only push it into another dimension. And how wonderful it is to have a place like the Peoria State Hospital, where that other dimension is so close all the time. History and ghost story are so intertwined at the asylum that sometimes it's not always easy to determine what are simply the echoes of the past and what are the activities of a phantom presence. We do know that there are circumstances that encourage paranormal activity on the hilltop. A shrill whistle was the "dinner bell", and that tends to get the spirits' attention. A whistle repeated three times was an alarm, meaning that a patient had wandered off of the grounds and needed to be found. Storms, too, will give people visiting the asylum a sense of urgency. An approaching storm sent the residents of the hilltop scurrying—it was everyone's job to help batten down the hatches as bad weather approached, making sure windows were closed, loose outdoor furniture secured, chickens brought safely in from the yard. Is this residual? Or is the sense of urgency being shared on purpose? All we know for sure is that the asylum is a place of wonder, both for those who love history and for those who love the paranormal.

The Peoria State Hospital, once you get to know her, is an easy place to love.

LAST THING:

"For more interactive fun, please scan these QR codes. The first code will take you to an audio tour of the hilltop. Listen to Sylvia narrate your walk as you discover the haunted hotspots of the Peoria State Hospital grounds. The second code will pull up the YouTube channel for the Pollak Hospital, where you'll find even more video and audio evidence. Enjoy!"

ACKNOWLEDGEMENTS

I am so very lucky to have a lot of talented, dedicated folks as friends and colleagues. I love history, and I love ghost stories, but I couldn't write a book on a place as intricate as the Peoria State Hospital all on my own. I had a lot of help.

I'm also very lucky to be in a place in my life where I can thank these people in public, in black and white. Thanks to Diane Lockhart, for seeing people most of us can't. Thanks to James Barrow, for seeing things from a different angle. And thanks to Christina Morris, for seeing past the last few years of the museum's existence to the rest of its inspiring history. These people's words made this book a richer experience for my readers, and I appreciate their help.

I also want to thank the paranormal investigators who shared their experiences for this book. A big thank you also goes to the volunteers at the Pollak Hospital, all of them—history, paranormal, and haunt. Thanks for all you do to keep the memories of the hilltop alive.

The biggest thanks of all go to my tolerant, wonderful husband Rob. Thanks for encouraging me to follow my dreams.

ABOUT THE AUTHOR

Sylvia Shults is the author of *44 Years in Darkness, Fractured Spirits: Hauntings at the Peoria State Hospital,* and other books of true ghost stories. She has spent the past twenty years working in a library, slowly smuggling words out in her pockets day by day to build a book of her own. She sits in dark, spooky, haunted places so you don't have to. She lives a short, ten-minute motorcycle ride away from the haunted asylum that features in so many of her books. She considers it the highest privilege to share the incredible, compassionate history of the Peoria State Hospital.

After battling an intense, lifelong fear of the dark, Sylvia decided to become a ghost hunter. (What WAS she thinking?) As a paranormal investigator, she has made many media appearances, including a tiny part in the Ghost Hunters episode "Prescription for Fear", about the Peoria State Hospital. She is a recurring guest on Ron Hood's podcast *Ron's Amazing Stories,* with the monthly segment "Ghost Stories With Sylvia". She is also the writer, director, producer, and host of the true ghost story podcast Lights Out, available on YouTube, iTunes, iHeart Radio, Spotify, and anywhere else great podcasts are found.

Sylvia loves hearing from her readers, especially when they have spooky stories of their own to share with her. She can be found at www.sylviashults.wordpress.com, and on Facebook at the pages for *Fractured Spirits* and *Ghosts of the Illinois River.*

Curious about other Crossroad Press books?
Stop by our site:
http://store.crossroadpress.com
We offer quality writing
in digital, audio, and print formats.

Made in the
USA
Lexington, KY